Still
Horsin'
Around

by
Don Coldsmith

Still
Horsin' Around

For Information address: Dancing Goat Press
3013 SW Quail Creek Dr., Topeka, Kansas 66614

PRINTING HISTORY
First Printing, June 2002
ISBN 0-9708160-2-2

Publisher's Cataloging-in-Publication

Coldsmith, Don, 1926-
    Still horsin' around / by Don Coldsmith. -- 1st ed.
    p. cm.
    ISBN 0-9708160-2-2

    1. Farm life--Middle West--Anecdotes. 2. Country
life--Middle West--Anecdotes. 3. Middle West--Social
life and customs--Anecdotes. 4. Coldsmith, Don, 1926-
I. Title.

S521.5.M53C56 2002   630'.977
                          QBI02-200432

Dancing Goat Press
Topeka, Kansas

PRINTED IN THE UNITED STATE OF AMERICA

Dedication

To my readers through the years, who are both contributors to and consumers of ***Horsin' Around***.

Introduction

Still Horsin' Around

In 1971, we were raising kids and horses, and I was beginning to write an occasional article for the horse magazines. I really had no ambitions to become a writer. I was asked by a friend, Merle Bird, editor of the small weekly *Emporia Times*, to write a weekly column about activities of the local and regional horse-oriented organizations. I wasn't very enthusiastic about it. I doubted that there was enough material to keep it going, but agreed to give it a try.

That was 30 years, nearly 1600 weekly columns ago. The *Emporia Times* was defunct within a year or so, for which I claim no credit. But, by that time, a couple of other papers were carrying the feature, "Horsin' Around." In the winter months, with horse activity pretty scarce, I'd write about something else. Now the feature has evolved (no offense to Creationists intended) into a general interest column. Some nostalgia, humor, country living, a little bit of everything. It's currently published in three states, and varies in distribution as we lose a subscribing paper or gain a couple more.

In 1975, an anthology of a hundred "Horsin' Around" columns was published in book form. The publisher took bankruptcy about 90 days later. Again, I take no responsibility. Only about 1,000 copies were ever circulated. Those are now high-dollar collector items. In 1981, another collection of assorted articles, *Horsin' Around Again* was moderately successful. But again, these volumes are now sought on the internet by collectors, at outrageous prices.

Meanwhile, I had started to write historical novels about the American West, now nearly forty books in number. Writing is now my full-time job. Well, except for our cattle operation. Readers of the Spanish Bit Saga and of the weekly columns have asked "When will you do another "Horsin' Around" book?" Okay, maybe it's time.

Still Horsin' Around is a collection of columns, mostly from the decade of the '90s. As before, not actually a horse book. But then, horsin' around doesn't necessarily have to involve horses, does it?

A number of people have told me that they keep one of the *Horsin' Around* books in the bathroom. They're in there just about long enough to read a page or two. Maybe three. Whatever works, I guess...

Hope you enjoy!

Don Coldsmith

At the time of the birth of the Horsin' Around column, Don was raising and showing Appaloosa horses, and acting as breed inspector for the APHC, the Appaloosa Horse Club of America. Breeders were encouraged to use the stylized horse logo on letterheads, in advertising, and on vehicles. It seemed logical to use it on a column titled Horsin' Around. Permission was asked and granted. Some subscibing papers have used the horse logo, some use a photo, some both, and some merely the Horsin' Around headline title.

The stylized Indian horse was designed in the 1950s by Dick Spencer III, for the Appaloosa organization. He was publisher of *Western Horseman* magazine, and wrote the introduction to the first Horsin' Around anthology. A few years ago he "crossed over," as his American Indian dad, Shatka Bearstep, would have said. He was a freind, and is surely missed.

DC

Ridin' for the Brand

When the kids were out of the nest, there were a lot fewer hands to gentle and halter-break new colts. We finally figured that there would be fewer colts if we stopped breeding mares. Close on the heels of this revelation came another idea. If we raised cattle instead we wouldn't have to halter-break any critters at all.

Our cow-calf operation produces about thirty calves a year. Our registered brand has been applied to a lot of calves, on the left hip location. A brand is read from left to right, and top to bottom. Consequently: "D C over quarter circle."

The brand will appear in this book from time to time when we have to put something in an extra patch of white space, not necessarily on the left hind quarter of the page.

D C

Table of Contents

Still
Horsin'
Around

by
Don Coldsmith

Silly Stuff, and Serious

Cat Fishin'

Everybody loves a good fish story. Some stories take on a life of their own, and we watch them come around again, in slightly different form, in a couple of years. This is not that sort of story. We know the people involved, the location of the fishing hole, and the circumstances. Although I was not present, I would personally vouch for the truth of this tale. At least, mostly. Names of the perpetrators have been changed, but the circumstances are guaranteed as described.

Again, mostly. We have no eyewitnesses, except for "Sam," who related the story, and his friend, "Raymond." Both are veteran fishermen. Their favorite fishing hole is a "whoop and a holler" behind Sam's house. He's an educated man, who is employed as a teacher. He also does some contracting, repair, and restoration on a custom basis. On the side, along with these other jobs, he operates a cow-calf operation on the ranch where he lives with his family. This is the location of the aforementioned fishing hole, a beautiful spring-fed pond with some depth to it, and a rocky shelf. Through the years he has worked at stocking the pond with the sort of fish he enjoys, fingerlings as well as an occasional fish caught elsewhere. There are both channel catfish and some of the big river cats there. Sam feeds them every evening with a bucket of commercial fish pellets. It's a pretty productive pond.

On the evening in question, the two friends carried their tackle down to the water's edge and began to rig their lines. Each would have two lines in the water, doubling their chances of a catch.

They moved apart a few yards, and Sam was still rigging his line when he heard Raymond's reel begin to sing as the line stripped rapidly from the spool.

Already? Sam looked over to where his partner was slipping and scrambling to regain control of his tackle. On the other end of fifty feet or so of heavy line was his catch, fighting mad, heading up the hill toward the barn. A large cat...No, not a cat-fish, but a barn cat. Raymond had baited his hook with a minnow and laid the rod down while he attached bait to his second rig. One of the many barn cats had followed the fishermen down the hill, spotted the minnow, and struck like a hungry channel cat.

Raymond tried to reel in his line, which wasn't easy with a furious, squalling and very active tom-cat on the other end. And the closer their proximity, the more activity and the louder the feline profanity. Sam grabbed a blanket from their pile of tack, and dropped it over the cat, hook, line, and sinker. The fight continued unabated, the noise somewhat muffled by the blanket.

Now as everyone knows, it is impossible to reason with a cat. When we call a dog, he'll usually answer. Call a cat, he'll take a message and get back to you later (if he feels like it). In this case, they now had a situation somewhat like an animated saguaro cactus wrapped in a thin blanket, screeching like a banshee and trying to destroy its rescuers. To turn loose would be sheer folly. The victim would emerge fightin' mad. Already, claws were raking through the blanket, seeking skin to lacerate.

At this point, some men might have used a large club to end the problem. Not these two. They're not only humane individuals, but they had no desire to try to explain to pet-loving wives and kids what happened to Sylvester. They may have figured that there was less risk to their own hides from the cat than from their families.

Cautiously, they unwrapped what appeared to be the front of the squirming bundle, converting the threat from claws to fangs. The squalling became louder. Incredibly, they managed to remove the hook from that cat's mouth without much loss of blood. Most of the blood, of course, was their own.

See you down the road.

Grass

People from other parts of the country often fail to understand our love of the prairie. Not all of them. Some fall in love with our grassland at first sight, recognizing the intricate and delicately balanced ecology, teeming with complicated life-forms. Others look at the rolling hills and see...Nothing. My grandfather, from whom I probably inherited my own love of the prairie, observed that "A man has to get out where he can stretch his eyes sometimes." (I'm sure he meant a woman, too. He used the term as in "mankind.")

Our tallgrass prairie really impressed some of the early mountain men. They described grass so tall that it could hide a rider on a big horse. You could ride out into the prairie, take a seed stalk from each side of your horse, and tie them together over the pommel of the saddle. I have read book reviews in which the reviewer scornfully rejected this description as a tall tale, suggesting that it must be a distorted description of a canebreak. The reviewer simply didn't understand. This can still be done, in a good year. I've done it. The grass involved is big bluestem, sometimes called turkeyfoot, one of the several grasses that make up the tallgrass prairie's environment.

Writers of the prairie environment have a tough time with copy editors in other parts of the country. Somebody who has never been west of New York doesn't realize that "tallgrass" is one word, not two. (The same with "panhandle," writers of the southern plains tell me.) I had once written an intense description of bluestem prairie, and the copy editor inserted a note in the margin: "Don't you mean bluegrass?" (No, dammit! There is no connection at all. In the eco-system we're talking about, bluegrass is a *weed*.) In fact, bluegrass is a cool-season grass, growing rapidly in spring and fall, and dormant in mid-summer. The prairie grasses are tropical in habit, and their most rapid growth to maturity and seed is in late summer. But to persons raised on concrete, grass is grass. They can look at a dozen species and not even realize the differences.

The term "grass" took on a bit of a different connotation a few years ago. Our kids' grandma was visiting, and showed the girls how to place a selected blade of grass between your thumbs and blow across it to make an interesting sound, much like the caw of a crow. I'd forgotten that we used to do that as kids. Some of the girls were pretty good at it, but we had to exercise a little caution. We didn't want the kids going to school relating that "My grandma blows grass, and she taught me to do it, too!"

But, back to tallgrass prairie. I think maybe the establishment of the Tallgrass Prairie Park at the Z-Bar Ranch may help to educate some of the outlanders. Some, of course, won't even be interested. They've *seen* grass, maybe in Central Park, and they know all about it. What's interesting about grass? Seen one patch, you've seen it all.

Even some who *think* they understand the situation don't have a clue. I heard from a reader in Kentucky a few months ago. He had read and enjoyed a couple of my books, and wanted to thank me. I'm always pleased at such a response, and so far, I try to answer each one with at least a note. This reader seemed to understand my approach to the cultural and racial conflicts in American history and my effort, in telling a story, to be fair about it.

He answered my thank-you note, which doesn't happen very often. I guess he'd read another book, maybe *Tallgrass*. He understood my love of the prairie, he said. He shared my feeling for the tallgrass country, because "more than ninety percent of Kentucky was originally tallgrass prairie."

Oh, boy, here we go again! Tallgrass prairie was strictly west of the Mississippi, in a strip from the Gulf of Mexico to Canada, only a hundred miles or so in width. He's still thinking in terms of bluegrass, which in our country is still a weed.

See you down the road.

Spider Bread

A few years ago we underwent some major changes in our household. Ever since we'd been married, we had a houseful of kids. Hers, mine, and ours; five in all. Edna stayed at home and handled that end, a full time job in itself.

But when the last of these girls went off to college, we were alone in the house for the first time. "What if we find out we don't even like each other?" Edna asked.

I think she wasn't really concerned about that, and it didn't become a problem. However, she did decide that she'd go back to work. She'd been teaching when we met, so she returned to the classroom, some twenty-five years later.

That, too, worked out pretty well. I was in the process of changing jobs. Changing professions, actually. I moved into writing full time. I converted one of the bedrooms into a study, built some shelving and cabinets, and tried to concentrate books and files from several areas into that one space. I'm still working on that. But consider...*She* became the one who gets up each morning to go to work, while I work at home.

All of our married life she had felt that the kitchen was *her* area. Except for Thanksgiving, of course, when I'd cook the turkey. When we'd cook out, the barbecue was mine. But basically, my presence in the kitchen wasn't tolerated well.

For a while after she went back to teaching, she'd try to come home and cook. Gradually I began to have something started, to relieve the load a little. The real turning point was one evening when she came home dead tired, and smelled the cheeseburgers on the stove. She admitted that it was nice, and granted permission to share the kitchen.

Now, what does a man cook? It's usually pretty limited. There's a cowboy saying that "if you can't cook it in a fryin' pan, it ain't worth eatin'." That's close, but not entirely true. I already had a jar of sourdough in the refrigerator, which provides pancakes occasionally. I worked on a chili recipe of my own for a couple of years, and finally got it like I want it. We always have some pretty good beef in the freezer, my other part-time job, so I had a lot to work with. Stews, soups, chowder. I began to experiment, and to clip recipes that looked quick and easy, mostly from *Grass and Grain*. They couldn't be too time-consuming, because I do have to write or research several hours a day, besides looking after cattle and all that goes with it.

Ann, my right-hand secretary/assistant, was getting a kick out of all this, and gave me my own recipe file box. I began to experiment. With the time limitation, the crock-pot turned out to be an ideal tool. I could start something in the morning and let it cook all day. I stumbled on an easy barbecue scheme: A layer of thin-sliced onions in the crock pot, then round steak, covered by a mix of equal parts of brown sugar, catsup, and picante sauce. Another layer of onions, steak, etc., cooked six or eight hours. We like it on hamburger buns.

If something works out pretty well, I send the recipe to our five daughters. Ann tries it too, of course. They all have their favorites. (The crock-pot barbecue is one.)

I have a pretty good idea now what will make a hit with a hungry wife when she lands here in the evening. Anything with sausage, bacon, cheese, potatoes, eggs, or onions can't go far wrong. Stew or chili on a cold night in the winter, and freeze part of the batch for another cold night.

No, I don't cook all the time. It depends on my schedule and hers. Sometimes I'm out of town for the day. Sometimes she gets home first. If worst comes to worst, we'll go out. Sometimes we do that anyway.

When I started to write this column, I had it in mind to write about an old-fashioned food called spider bread. No, not made with spiders. "Spider" is a frontier name for a cast iron skillet. Sourdough bread can be cooked over a campfire by turning it once in the spider, or skillet. The recipe I had didn't work. It tasted good, but fell apart when I turned it. I'll try again.

Good lord! I've written a recipe column.

See you down the road.

Misprints, Gallbladders & Patchboxes May 1993

Any writer makes some errors. It is only to be hoped that they aren't big ones. There are inside jokes among writers about the time somebody who should have known better simply got careless.

One well known western writer (no, not L'Amour) once had his hero crouch behind a rock and quietly slip the safety off his revolver. (Hint: a revolver has no safety latch, but uses the half-cock position as a safe.) That's the sort of thing that's a constant hazard, and will have the writer's colleagues and friends joking about it for years.

This sort of error is in addition to the familiar "typos" and printing errors. In the production of a book, there are at least a half dozen people besides the author who read and edit. Editors, copy editors, proof readers…And the author sees it at least twice more after he finishes it, once as edited manuscript, again as proof galley.

Imagine my surprise, then, when one of my students recently called attention to a printing error in the very first paperback of the Spanish Bit series. A silly thing. The text is referring to the daughter of one of the main characters. A one-letter mistake, substituting an "l" for a "d." Daughter becomes "laughter," which makes no sense at all. But here's the odd thing: That book is in the eleventh printing, and nobody seems to have noticed. The word is so obviously supposed to be "daughter" that the reader (as well as the author, editor, copy editors, proof readers, etc.) all read it as it should be, not as it is.

My biggest real mistake, which I've mentioned before, was probably in about my fifth book. I described in detail the butchering of a deer, including the careful removal of the gallbladder. It was several years before a veterinarian reader contacted me about the fact that a deer does not have a gallbladder. I always thought everything had a gallbladder! With the help of a friend who is a biologist (but didn't know either, at first) I finally learned that there are a few mammals that do not. Deer, rats, horses, and "sometimes giraffes," the textbook said. This is crazy, I thought. All of these have close relatives with gallbladders…And on a giraffe, it's optional equipment?

Well, I've gotten a lot of mileage out of the story, telling it as a part of one of my lectures on the Kansas Humanities Council circuit.

Recently, I received a note from another veterinarian, who had heard that lecture. He had just learned, he said, that there's another class of mammals without gallbladders, the "camelidae." With people raising exotic pets like llamas, vicunas, guanacos, and alpacas, this becomes important. At least to veterinarians, I guess. I doubt that any of my characters will attempt to butcher a llama, though.

Recently, a friend saved me from a mistake equally bad. In the upcoming book, *Thunderstick*, I had a scene where the character took cloth patches out of the brass-covered compartment in the stock of his musket. It's called the patchbox. My editor happened to send a copy of the unedited proof galleys to one of the Kansas Muzzleloaders I'd met in February. That was fortunate, because there was an error. One that would not be noticed except by one reader in a thousand, but I'd worry about that one. If an author doesn't strive for accuracy, he (or she) loses credibility. Readers who are informed will snicker about his ignorance.

Even admitting that there are glaring errors made by Pulitzer winners like James Michener, I'd be embarrassed if my muzzleloader friend hadn't caught this one. He phoned me to point out that in the time frame of the book, this would have to be a French musket, which would not have a patchbox. Anyway, we did catch it in time, I think...

See you down the road.

Alas, the Carnage
August 2001

The family from Texas had been visiting relatives in Emporia, and were starting home, about 5:30 PM. They headed west on Highway 50, but before they had even gotten up to speed, it was apparent that there was trouble ahead.

An accident, involving several cars, crushed and damaged beyond recognition. At least one had apparently burned, and a couple of others were tossed and strewn across the highway for fifty yards or so. There was debris…Broken wheels, burned tires, strips of chrome, broken glass, littering the whole area. Surely, one of the worst chain-reaction accidents ever, judging from the number of demolished vehicles.

The conversation in the Texans' car apparently went something like this:

"My god! Look at that!"

"Totally crushed! Do you suppose the semi rolled over on them?"

"That one's burned."

"Yeah, that one, too! Such carnage!"

"There are going to be bodies," said Grandma. "I'm not even going to look!"

"But where are the ambulances? The emergency vehicles?"

"Who's helping the injured?"

"Don't they *care* here in Kansas?"

"No sirens, even?"

***

Now, let us skip to the next day. After the Texans reached home, they phoned the Emporia relatives to report on the trip. Naturally, after assuring Sis that they had arrived safely, they began to recount the trauma they had witnessed as they left Emporia. Carnage beyond belief, debris and destruction strewn everywhere.

But the reaction on the part of the relative at the Emporia end was completely unexpected. The woman was actually roaring with uncontrolled laughter! Not only that, but the more lurid the description became, the harder she laughed. Had she lost her mind completely?

Not exactly…But, through one of those odd quirks of circumstance and coincidence, she had already heard the same story, but from another angle, through a friend of a friend.

***

In this version, a local citizen from Emporia was returning home from Topeka, about 5:30. He left the Turnpike, circled back west toward his rural home, and entered Highway 50. Ahead of him was a large flatbed truck, with a load piled high. The load appeared a bit too tall and possibly unsteady, and something told him to be careful. He backed off, pulled over, and actually stopped on the shoulder of the highway at about the same time that the crash occurred.

Debris fell all around him, wheels and tires and flying parts of automobiles. He figured that he was one of the luckiest of drivers that day, to have avoided injury and damage to his own vehicle, and his own hide. He managed to make his way on home, where, pale and shaken, he recounted his adventures to his wife.

She called a friend, who retold it to her spouse, and on to yet another friend. As luck would have it, out of 30,000 people in the area, that one happened to be the sister of the Texan who had been visiting her.

Thus, it came to pass that when he called to relate the trauma they had experienced, the sister already knew the rest of the story. How, in fact, the salvage truck had been piled too high with cars headed for recycling. It had struck the overpass bridge, knocking and scattering the load of crushed vehicles up and down the highway and ditches.

She knew that her brother was stringing her along with tales of carnage. That there had been no injuries. Only one human being was directly involved…The unfortunate driver of the salvage truck, who certainly had a problem. But, no carnage. The accident didn't even rate space in the local paper.

See you down the road.

Cats and Jelly-Bread   August 1993

Everybody knows about Murphy's Law, which states that if any-thing can go wrong, it will. There are dozens of spinoffs and correlar-ies to fit different situations. Did you ever realize, for instance, that automotive finishes attract shopping carts magnetically? The more recent the model-year, the greater the magnetic pull. Apparently the attraction begins to leak out in a year or two, like a dying flashlight bat-tery. In a matter of ten years or so, there's virtually no attraction left.

There's a scientific journal called *The Journal of Irreproducible Results*. It's devoted entirely to subjects like the above. Many of the articles are generated by actual scientific experiments which went wrong, ruining the project. A classic example, of course, is that of Alexander Fleming, of London. In 1928, Fleming saw that colonies of bacteria in his laboratory had been ruined by contamination with green mold. Most of us would have pitched out the whole experiment. He was clever enough, however to realize the importance of his observa-tion. The mold was killing the bacteria, and he had just discovered penicillin.

Usually, such oddball happenstances do not lead to such lofty results, though. At this time of year there is usually a flurry of reports of gardeners who found a potato shaped like the state of Florida, or a tomato that looks like Rush Limbaugh. Of course, most tomatoes do.

I once saw a TV segment about a lady who had a collection of potato chips that look like something else. Flowers, animals, trees, a rocking chair…She had an edge on any other potato chip collector, however, since she was an inspector on the line at a potato chip facto-ry. Of one thing, I'm certain. She has no teenagers at home.

Speaking of kids reminds me of a rather bizarre contest that was carried out for readers of the scientific magazine *Omni* recently. It was strictly for fun, and involved a lot of nonsensical "irrepro-ducible results." One of the suggestions that proved a winner dealt with the tendency of a buttered slice of bread to land buttered side down when dropped.

Since that virtually always happens, and a dropped cat always lands on its feet, let's combine those two basic forces. Tie a slice of bread, butter side up, to the back of a cat, suggested their reader, and drop it. The opposing forces will counteract each other and the unit will hover indefinitely in mid-air. The suggestion was made that this principle of levitation could be harnessed to operate hover-craft.

Now, let's get serious. The *Omni* reader who came up with that idea is a rank amateur, dealing with rudimentary ideas. Anyone who has raised five kids, as we have, knows that there are other variables at work here. Jelly, or better still, peanut butter and jelly would be ever so much more effective than mere butter. Then it's also true that the bread will *almost* always land spread-side down. It's not infallible. There's another variant at work. The odds of jelly-side down vary directly with the cost of the carpet.

But, the idea does, after all, have merit. I can visualize a transportation system based on this theory. Hover-craft could travel over a roadway of carpet of varying cost, depending on which areas were found to be in need of greater levitation.

Platoons of cats with jelly-bread strapped on their backs would be rotated in shifts of a few hours each. Compartments under each car would be filled with these hover-cats. They would work for a few hours and then have their little harnesses removed to rest and eat until their next shift.

This finds useful homes for all the stray cats now being euthanized in pounds. It provides jobs, not only for those who will work in the…uh…cat-house, but for those who grow the fruit to make the jelly…Hey! Maybe economic recovery is in sight!

See you down the road.

Hey, Coach   August 2001

Football season is upon us once again, and there will be dozens of interviews with coaches. There will be, especially at college level, the "rankings." I'm always at a loss as to how it's possible to rank the standings of teams which have never played yet. But, that's part of the job of the sportswriter, a pretty tough job at best.

I've devised a labor-saving device which may make that job easier. How about a standardized form or two, in which the questions asked the coach are pre-answered? It will save the coach's time, as well as that of the journalist:

Well, coach (insert name), your (insert team mascot or symbol) have their season opener this (insert day of week). What can you tell us?

Well, (insert sportswriter's nickname) the (insert opposing team's mascot) will be comin' down here to play ball. We'll have to be ready for 'em. They have a good team and a great coach.

Yes, I understand you and coach (insert opposing coach's name) are old friends. Worked together?

Yes, we were assistants under coach (insert former boss's name) at (insert name of university where previously employed).

But what about your team here. Are you ready?

Well, we've got some work to do. A little trouble with injuries. We'll be ready to play, though.

Who's your starting quarterback?

Not really sure, (insert interviewer's nickname). Both (insert QB name) and (insert other QB) are executing well. We'll decide by game time.

Any particular strategy against the (insert opponent's mascot)?

Well, we'll have to execute well, and not make any mistakes.

How about their offense?

We've been lookin' at tapes. (Insert opponent's QB) did some good work last season when their starter was injured. We'll have to anticipate, have our defense ready to play ball.

And your offense?

Well, we'll try a couple of things. Ready to change if we need to.

Well, thanks for the interview, coach. Have a good season!

***

Well you get the idea. About three basic forms will do it. The one above and two more, one for use after a loss:

Well, (insert interviewer's name), they came to play and we didn't. We've got to anticipate, and execute better. But the (opponent's mascot) have a fine football team. They deserved to win. We have some work to do.

Or after a win: Well, (insert interviewer's name), we were able to win today over a fine football team, well coached. Our (insert home team's mascots) worked hard and deserved to win. But of course, we still have some work to do before we meet (insert next opponent).

***

You can probably tell, this season, whether any of the sportswriters are using my pre-printed forms. Watch for them.

Seriously, though, my hat's off to the coach. I could never do his job, and all the jokes about dumb athletes and dumb coaches would really bother me. They *have* to be quick.

Think about it…In a league with say, ten teams…The coach has a statistical chance of one in ten for a championship season. Only a fifty-fifty chance of even a winning season. And, any season that finds the Podunk University Oysters below that halfway mark will probably have the alumni hollering for the coach's scalp.

So, my hat's off to the guy with one of the toughest jobs in the world. I couldn't live like that. Whatever he's paid, he *earns*, in blood, sweat, and tears.

Sure, college football is commercialized, but it does turn out some fine young athletes, and some fine young men. I really hate to see any of them get into trouble. And some do…Some kids are going to do that in spite of anything. But it always gives me a good feeling to read about a top college athlete who also has a top grade point average. I know we'll hear about him for a long time. And his coach will be proud.

See you down the road.

Scholastically Ineligible

Some time ago I wrote about visiting a college campus in another part of the country. Their athletic boosters club was selling banners and various booster artifacts with a major grammatical error. I was astonished that the team was referred to as the "Bulldog's." (That's not the real name. I've harassed that school enough, and carried on some correspondence with their Department of English, which disclaims any connection with Athletics. Rightly so. This was a major, state-operated university. Surely, anyone with even a high school English course should have known that a team name with a mascot like the bulldog are the Bulldogs, not Bulldog's.)

I'm afraid this is all part of the rapid dumbing down of America. I read recently that the latest Webster dictionary contains 300 new words. What's the point, when we can't handle the ones we have? I blame part of it on the computer's spell-check, which only tells whether it's a *word*, not whether it's correct. But how many college graduates are carrying banners proclaiming their illiteracy? Quite a few.

Every Monday, Jay Leno's program features a segment of stupid headlines from around the country. He never runs out of material.

But it's not just headlines…Sometimes it's merely misuse of everyday words, such as the "Bulldog's," or putting on the "breaks." (*Brakes*, I suppose.) A couple of years ago, I started a file folder of "stupidity in print," major errors clipped from any publication I happen to encounter. Now I'm not claiming my own infallibility. Sure, I make mistakes, which may be pointed out to me with great glee by my spouse or my secretary, either or both. But I try. My file folder, however, grows fatter. In the past few weeks, the summer sports season, I have clipped more than *thirty* examples of the "Bulldog's" mistake from sports pages. I finally gave up on that one.

There's a long-standing school of humor about dumb jocks and scholastic eligibility. For example, the star player's grades aren't up to par, and the administration agrees to a special exam, tests in English, History, and Math.

The English test consists of writing his full name, which he can do. Historically, he guesses the name of the public figure who rests in Grant's tomb. But he's not sure on Math...Two plus three...After a struggle, he blurts out "five!"

Just then the coach intervenes. "Aw, come on, Professor, can't you give him another chance?"

This is a cheap shot, of course. Much like mother-in-law jokes, or lawyer jokes. (How many lawyer jokes are there? Just one...The rest are true accounts.) But I digress.

Everybody surely realizes that a successful coach has to be pretty smart. He deals not only with players, but with the public, the media, the alumni, the administration, the sportswriters, the Monday morning quarterbacks, the odds-makers and poll-takers...

And, that's only the *people* that he has to deal with. He has to contend with weather, with schedules, techniques, ever-changing rules and theories, systems, the sheer mechanics of putting a couple dozen fine athletes up against somebody else's squad, maybe equal or better. I really admire some of the young men who can handle a sports season, maintain their grades, sometimes with a wife and family too. That is a well-rounded individual. An athlete with a 3-something grade average might not even make such mistakes as calling his team the "Bulldog's."

A thought occurs to me...Could it be that it's not the jocks and coaches who are illiterate? Maybe it's the sports *writers*. I do have a bulging file folder of evidence...I'm on thin ice, here. I have a number of good friends who are journalists. At least, I did have until I wrote this piece. A writer with writer friends is quite vulnerable. *They* can write about *him* (her) too. In this case, I especially miss a brother of mine, who died several years ago. He was a writer...A sports writer for a while. Also, a war correspondent, an editor of World Book encyclopedia, and worked for Associated Press. Probably his first love was sports writing, though. I miss him, and wish he was here now. I'd really have some stuff with which to harass him.

Go, Bulldog's!

See you down the road.

Grandma's Shoes

September 2001

When I was very little all the grandmas that I knew,
  were wearing the same kind, of ugly grandma shoe.
You know the kind I mean, clunky heeled, black, lace-up kind.
  They looked so very awful, that it weighed upon my mind.
For I knew when I grew old, I'd have to wear those shoes.
  I'd think of that from time to time, it seemed like such bad news.
I never was a rebel. I wore saddle shoes to school.
  And next came ballerinas, then the sandals, pretty cool.
And then came spikes with painted toes, then platforms, very tall.
  As each new fashion came along, I wore them one and all.
But always in the distance, looming in my future there,
  was that awful pair of ugly shoes, the kind that grandmas wear.
I eventually got married, and then became a mom.
  Our kids grew up and left, and when their children came along,
I knew I was a Grandma and the time was drawing near,
  when those clunky, black, old lace-up shoes was what I'd have
  to wear.
How would I do my gardening or take my morning hike?
  I couldn't even think about how I would ride my bike!
But fashions kept evolving and one day I realized,
  that the shape of things to come was changing, right before
  my eyes.
And now when I go shopping, what I see fills me with glee.
  For in my jeans and Reeboks I'm comfy as can be.
And I look at all these little girls and there, upon their feet,
  are clunky, black, old grandma shoes and I really think that's neat.

(Author unknown)

***

I ran across this poem some time ago. I'd like to give credit to whoever wrote it, but there's no good way to find out. It's just one of those things which drift around, turning up in various places and circumstances. But it's very well done, and speaks volumes about our culture.

For some reason, each generation seems to choose a few things about the past to ridicule. I suppose teenagers have always been embarrassed by their parents. They don't seem to realize that it's a two-way street. But in the past few years the gap between the generations has become virtually self-destructive on the part of the teens. If they had been forced to endure the clothing, shoes, music, food, and mutilation of their bodies that passes for normal just now, they'd be hollering child abuse. And, rightly so.

But back to footwear...Shoes, as we know them, are comparatively recent. Before the "Civil" War, it was rare to even have right and left. They were interchangeable, both made on the same "flat last." Ladies' shoes, of course, went by a separate set of rules. The main requirement, as I understand it, was that such footwear must in no way resemble the foot of a woman. This requirement is still in effect.

Back to granny shoes, though...When I was a very small kid, our maternal grandma came to live with us. She had a nice lap, and a comfortable rocking chair. She'd read to us, or sing a lullaby (in German) to lull us to sleep. There came a time when she needed new shoes, and my dad took her over to the shoe store. She scandalized everybody by buying, not a clunky old pair of grandma shoes, but a pair of brown and white saddle oxfords like the teenagers were wearing. She even wore them to church. She figured that at her age, she should be able to wear any shoes she wanted, and my folks backed her up on it. In retrospect, she was a pretty independent sort of woman for that day and age, and she loved those shoes. She'd have been buried in them, I guess, except I doubt she was wearing shoes. She also wanted special music at her funeral: Sousa's "Stars and Stripes Forever." Unfortunately, she didn't get her way on that, either.

See you down the road.

Naked, Nekkid, and Nude July 1996

There's probably no one who hasn't at some time or other had an embarrassing dream about this. You suddenly find yourself on the street, in a classroom, at a party, or at work, with no clothes on. You waken in terror, and for a minute or two, halfway between the dream world and the real world, there's a shadow of doubt. *Did it really happen?*

Afterward, it's funny. (That is, if it *was* only a dream. If not, you're probably reading the wrong column.)

The other day I was listening to the radio in the pickup, and chanced on a program about words. I've always been fascinated by words; their origins, meanings, and usages. This lady was talking about "nude" and "naked", which at first glance would seem to mean the same thing. But not really, she insisted. There are subtle differences here, which we don't really stop to notice under most circumstances.

Both words apparently go back originally to Latin, where "nudus" meant exactly what we might suspect: Nude or naked. By the time it became an Anglo-Saxon word, it was "nacod," meaning the same thing.

But in the dictionary, some differences begin to show up. "Naked" has some added meanings, such as helpless, defenseless, unassisted. In the field of astronomy, for example, "naked eye" means with no lenses or telescopes. Another subtle meaning: The uncovering of that which is customarily covered, as in "a naked sword." All of these usages seem to hint at something threatening or unavoidable. Something that wasn't really wanted. "Stripped naked" surely has an unpleasant connotation.

Nude, on the other hand, invokes a certain amount of free will. "Nudes" in art are considered perfectly acceptable. Many, even highly desirable. There are "nude beaches" in parts of the world where people who prefer skinny-dipping to some of the ridiculous attire seen on other beaches may do so unfettered. By *choice*. Nudist camps or colonies are populated by those who choose to be there. So, "nude" begins to appear as if there is free choice involved, while "naked" implies misfortune or accident, or worse.

I would be remiss if I didn't mention "naked as a jaybird." As far as I know, jaybirds seem no more naked than any other avian species. Why not "naked as a buzzard" or a chickadee or ostrich? Some things, I guess, are simply not intended to be understood.

I'm sure, also, that there will be those who will disapprove of my choice of topics for this column. My grandmother would have been shocked. She always had trouble talking about fried chicken, because the leg, thigh, (and even worse), corresponded to the names of human body parts. I'm sorry, Grandma…You're right, and if God had meant us to run around naked, we'd have probably been born that way.

More seriously, haven't our ways changed since my grandmother was a girl well over a century ago? I could not have submitted a column like this to a family newspaper then. It would have been scandalous. I might have been stripped naked, tarred and feathered.

By contrast, a few years ago there was an award-winning novel with the title *The Nekkid Cowboy*. I'm sure the title made people want to read the book, because it sounds a little bit naughty…Not *too* much.

I don't know exactly how the Americanized and Westernized term "nekkid" relates to Latin and Anglo-Saxon roots, but I did get a clue. This was from an old cowboy who was commenting on that book's title.

"Well, 'naked' means you got no clothes on. 'Nekkid' means you got no clothes on, and you're up to somethin'."

See you down the road.

The Weather Stick   May 2001

Some friends recently gave us an interesting instrument with which to predict the weather. It's called a Woodsman's Weather Stick.

At first I was inclined to regard it as a joke. There are a lot of gag gifts out there, many based on puns or quirks in the strange language we call English. A "chain saw": a length of light chain stretched in a hacksaw frame...) A "three piece chicken dinner": (three grains of yellow corn in a little box.) And there are a lot of weather indicators. I've seen a short length of cotton rope nailed to a stick: If the rope is wet, it's rainy. If dry, it's clear. If warm, it's sunny. If blowing out horizontally, it's windy. If frozen, icy, and so on. Such things are actually sold.

On closer examination, it appeared that maybe the weather stick is intended to be taken seriously. It comes from the state of Maine, which certainly has been noted for some of its backwoods qualities for a long time. Not that there is anything wrong with backwoods wisdom, however. We're deluded sometimes by the flood of new technology with which we're constantly bombarded. "New and improved" are not necessarily inseparable. I've always subscribed to the theory "If it ain't broke, don't fix it."

I recently saw a TV segment about the excessive cost of ATMs. (For my fellow dinosaurs, that's an automatic teller machine, by means of which one may extract his own cash from a machine on the street, for a fee. Often, an exorbitant fee.) Now wouldn't it be almost as easy to write a check or even carry a little money? I'd guess that the occasions when one is suddenly confronted with the completely unexpected need for cash are pretty rare. A little forethought would eliminate such a crisis. Maybe there's very little forethought any more. But just because a high-tech capability exists, there's an urge to use it. An old timer once asked me "Do you think radio was really improved by the addition of pictures?" He had a point. Sometimes our complete dependence on such luxuries as electricity makes me a bit uneasy, and I don't even live in California.

Everyone has a tendency to believe that until his own generation: A) There was no high-tech knowledge whatever, B) No one had a sense of humor, and C) Sex had not yet been discovered. Obviously, all of these assumptions are false, or we wouldn't even be here.

Civilization has probably lost or forgotten more high-tech knowledge than we have now. How did Vikings navigate without a compass? Is the compass really better than what they had? I've also heard that in the recording industry, many experts concede that the very best quality is not in tape or CDs, but in the old wax discs. This probably doesn't matter, because a whole generation will soon be deaf from the sheer volume of what they listen to. (I'll not stoop to call it music.)

But our grandparents used high-tech methods to make soap and cure hams. Is it significant at all that soap like Grandma's sells for higher prices than modern harsh detergents? Or that country-cured hams are much preferred over the taste-free waterlogged product we have now?

Back to the old woodsman's weather stick...Does it work? We'll see...It's a bone-dry twig, of unknown species from Maine, said to have been used by the Abanaki Indians to foretell weather. In damp weather, it absorbs humidity from the air and droops. When it dries, it stands more erect. It depends, then, on humidity in the air. With such supporting data and careful observation of other factors, they could probably do a pretty good job of forecasting. Maybe there are some mystical qualities, like that of the "water witch" with a witch hazel branch.

As I write this, I'm watching the weather stick from time to time. I tacked it up outside the screen porch, where we can see it from the kitchen window. The stick was dry as dust when it came out of the commercial package, and had a sharp upturn to its shape. The day is overcast and humid, foggy earlier, but not raining. Humidity seems quite high.

It's been about two hours since I put the stick on the post according to directions. It was pointing sharply upward. The tip of the twelve-inch, slender twig has moved through an arc of about 30 degrees, maybe ten inches. It's drooping below horizontal now, and the weather man predicts 30 percent chance of rain.

See you down the road.

The Brown Grand Theater April 1996

A century ago every small town in the Midwest probably saw itself as the nucleus of a booming city. But whether they did or not, each was aware of the importance of education and culture. The institutions that caused a town to grow and prosper were law enforcement, followed closely by churches and schools. Culture. Many early settlers were illiterate, of course, but some were highly educated. Cowboys often had access to paperback editions of classic literature, distributed as premiums by Arbuckle Coffee. Some of the mountain men of the fur trade era were even known to quote Shakespeare.

So, it should not be unexpected that many Kansas towns had a theater. This was long before movie theaters. We're talking about stage plays and concerts and recitals. In a lot of towns this was known as the Opera House.

Not long ago, I was in Concordia, Kansas, helping with a writing seminar at Cloud County Community College, one of the fine two year colleges in the state. The people with whom I was working insisted that I must tour the Brown Grand Theater. They even picked me up at the Bed and Breakfast where I stayed (another great experience) to take me downtown to the Theater.

I was really impressed. It was like stepping back through time about a century to the Victorian elegance that we've allowed to slip away. The Brown Grand Theater was built in 1906 and 1907, by a prominent citizen, Col. Napoleon Bonaparte Brown. Actual supervision of the construction was carried out by the Colonel's son, Earl. Total cost was $40,000, a major expenditure at the time. The architecture and decor are French Renaissance. The Theater seats 650 people, with two large balconies and eight box seats, which are on two levels. There were private entrances for the box seats, so that the holders of the first class tickets didn't even have to mingle with the public.

A magnificent reproduction of a famous painting by Horace Vernet, "Napoleon at Austerlitz," adorned the grand drape stage curtain. Earl Brown had commissioned the curtain as a surprise gift for his father, Napoleon.

The opening performance was on September 17, 1907, a play entitled "The Vanderbilt Cup." From that time until 1925, the theater provided not only legitimate theater by touring companies, but also local talent, lectures, vaudeville, and even "wrestling and boxing exhibitions."

In 1925, the theater was sold to the Concordia Amusement Company. Live theater was being threatened by a new entity, the "moving picture." A projection booth was constructed in the rear of the second balcony, and a new era had begun. Silent films with Harold Lloyd and Charlie Chaplin and Rudolph Valentino graced the screen. It was not until four years later that movies began to talk.

Meanwhile, the Brown Grand continued to be used for live entertainment too. Like many theaters, they sometimes had live acts between movies or during an "intermission." After half a century as a movie house, the last movie was shown there in 1974.

A renovation and restoration was begun shortly after. There had been a lot of water damage after a tornado tore off a part of the roof in 1967. The grand drape curtain was destroyed. It was discovered, however, that the same company who had painted Napoleon in 1907, was still in business in Minneapolis. They painted another like it for a new grand drape in the late 1970s.

After the restoration, at more than ten times the total cost of the original construction, the Brown Grand Theater held a new grand opening on September 17, 1980, exactly 73 years after the original. Fittingly, the same play, "The Vanderbilt Cup" was the featured offering. Guests of honor were three local ladies who had attended the original opening in 1907, as small children. This time they had box seats.

The Brown Grand is used, too. There are more than 70 events each year…A variety of local and regional events, the schools and college, church and other organizations…It's a great performing arts center as well as a tourist attraction. Well worth the time for a guided tour. (A dollar donation requested, hours 9-12 and 1-4 daily, Sundays 1-4).

See you down the road.

DC

This Little Piggie

June 1993

"This little piggie went to market..." We don't hear that children's rhyme much any more. It's a part of our culture that's being neglected. I suppose that there are a lot of households where it's still in use. Parents or grandparents or even daycare people play with little ones, read to them, and carry on the traditional riddles and rhymes that are part of our culture. Part of our education, actually. The folk stories, songs, and rhymes were valuable teaching tools to help prepare a child for life as a part of the adult world.

It took me a long time to realize that all these nonsensical little ditties actually make sense, when considered in their original context. "This little piggie..." The big toe, the fattest, is ready for market. The second toe, long and slim "stayed home." It needs to be fatter before it will bring a good price. The next toe: "This little piggie ate roast beef," indicates an animal that eats everything eagerly, while the fourth, which "ate none" is much smaller, not even ready to fatten yet. The fifth toe is a baby, still crying "wee-wee-wee, all the way home" in the high-pitched squeal of a tiny piglet. There, in a few humorous lines, was a practical lesson for a child who in a few years would be raising pigs.

A similar exercise done with the hands was recalled to me by a small granddaughter recently. It starts with hands folded, fingers interlaced and inside closed fists. "This is the church, and this is the steeple..." (Index fingers raised, tips together, to form a steeple.) "Open the doors and see all the people." Both hands are opened and inverted to show rows of fingers representing people in church pews. This implied to a child that going to church is good and is expected.

There's a second benefit here, too. The repetitive motion teaches dexterity. Inexperienced little fingers learn to respond skillfully. Similarly, "patty-cake" games not only tell something about baking, but help eye and hand coordination.

My German grandmother had a number of these little games. One, of which I'm not certain about the origin, was a rhyme similar to "This little piggie," but done on the fingers. I believe that it had two purposes. One was to encourage the use of the hands and improve coordination. The other seems a bit more subtle, but let's consider:

"Five little froggies, all in a row..." (Fingers of course.)

"This little froggie broke his toe." (The little finger, extended and bent.)

"This little froggie (middle finger) laughed and was glad,

This little froggie (index finger) cried and was sad.

But this little froggie, (thumb) kind and good, hopped after the doctor as fast as he could."

The thumb was then flexed rapidly with a jerking, hopping motion, It could be done in reverse, with the little finger doing the hopping, but it's harder and requires more coordination.

It was years later before I realized the real message in that little exercise. It's a course in emergency management. There are four possible reactions to an emergency, depicted in that little game: panic (oh! oh! oh!) lack of sympathy (laughed and was glad) ineffective sympathy (cried and was sad). But the sensible reaction is the one that depicts help for an injured companion. Any child identifies with the sensible frog who goes for help.

These little childhood exercises went a long way to establish priorities and basic life adjustments. They turned out pretty capable people, with coordination, ethics, and an understanding of human interactions. This form of education was very important. We can only hope that it continues in some families. And, I hope that they'll get some of the same from anthropomorphic amphibians and fuzzy pink heroes on the idiot box.

See you down the road.

It's a Misteak April 1993

A few years ago there was a movie release whose very title caused a ripple of chuckles around the country. "Attack of the Killer Tomatoes." It was a good-natured spoof of the many science fiction movies of the 1950s, and had some state of the art special effects. It never won any Oscars or became a classic, except in a cult sense.

Now I have an idea for a movie along these lines, based not on the dangers of atomic mutation but more current threats. My story, too, would be a spoof. It would be about an oddly organized group of environmental extremists, fanatic vegetarians ("Vegans"), and terrorist groups who think that all animals have the same "rights" as humans. (Not animal welfare, to which we all subscribe, but *rights*. No animal to be "exploited" for human use, ever.)

This group announces that they intend to take over control of America's future by altering everyone's diet. Their contention is that all the evils in the history of mankind can be blamed on the eating of meat. No reputable scientists will support their simplistic theories, but this matters not to the activists. All they need is an *enemy* to get public attention.

They select an old and respected fast-food chain, and decide to force the adoption of their idea: Stop using meat and convert, for their time-honored sandwich, to a patty of ground vegetables. They will enforce this by picketing. (I haven't quite figured how to do this. Don't these fanatics have homes and jobs? Well, a minor problem for a movie script...)

Somehow, I haven't gotten many film producers interested in this scenario. It's too far out, apparently. About as believable as the Killer Tomatoes. But are you ready for the scary part? It is all *true*. The organization is "Beyond Beef," based on the title of a book by Jeremy Rifkin. Their enemy is McDonald's, and they intend to picket, starting April 17, 1993, demanding adoption of their (ugh!) "Veggie-burger."

A closer look reveals that Mr. Rifkin appears to have no academic credentials in science, medicine, nutrition, or agriculture, yet he criticizes those who do. His track record includes such widely divergent efforts as attempting to stop the space program, all beef production, sex education, and all genetic engineering research. His theories have been refuted by virtually every respected scientific research organization in the United States. Officers of the Audubon Society, who once looked at Rifkin with lukewarm interest, have now disavowed any support. Cornell University researchers have disproved his statements about ozone layer destruction. (Oh, yes, McDonald's caused that, too!) The American Dietetic Association has joined in a Food Facts Coalition with seventeen other respected organizations to combat the bizarre misinformation purveyed by these extremists.

Naturally, McDonald's will fight, as they should. I have no connection there, but McDonald's deserves public support.

One really scary thought: Some "animal rights" groups who are *not* connected with Rifkin and Beyond Beef but support Rifkin and his ideas: PETA, "People for Ethical Treatment of Animals." Their top level leadership people were indicted by a grand jury last fall for terrorist activities. Another, ALF, the "Animal Liberation Front" is listed by the FBI as a terrorist group.

These are the people who bomb research labs, "free" lab, zoo and domestic animals to run loose on freeways, and have destroyed years of data on animal diseases at university research labs.

So, what to do? It wouldn't hurt to eat an extra Big-Mac (or any other hamburger).

Meanwhile, back to my movie version: What about a title? "Beyond *Belief*"? Or maybe it would be better to name it after the (ugh!) Veggie-burger: How about THE MISTEAK?

See you down the road.

The Recipe Column September 1994

A few months ago I wrote a column about how I started to do a bit more cooking at home. Edna was teaching, and it seemed logical for me to start fixing supper, because I work at home. I told about what sorts of things I'd cook. Hamburgers, eggs, the sort of stuff a mere man could cook in a skillet. Pretty easy stuff, really.

I even shared a recipe, one I created for an easy barbecue in a crock pot. By the time I finished the 600 words or so, I realized that I'd written a recipe column. I was startled, and commented on it.

I wasn't really prepared for the reaction. I received several letters about it, and a lot more comments in person. People had enjoyed it and it was fun. One reader suggested that I branch out, adding a regular feature called "Horsin' Around in the Kitchen." (I'd better not comment on the possibilities there.)

Several people mentioned the barbecue recipe. One lady in Florida wrote that her husband had tried it. She explained that they, as a couple, had always had the gender role reversal situation. There are an increasing number of men who like to cook. Of course, some are famous chefs. I found quite a few men who cook regularly at least part of the time. ("He's a better cook then I am," several women told me.)

The real shocker came in August, though, in a letter from one of the small town papers where my column appears. Local people there had enjoyed my recipe article. Some had tried the barbecue "several times," the editor said. Now I'd been nominated for "Meet the Cook," a weekly feature in their paper which highlights local and area cooks.

Well, I was honored, but shocked of course. I don't really take myself too seriously. The newspaper sent a form with questions about who inspired my interest in cooking, what types of foods are my favorites to prepare, and a suggestion that I recount my most "surprising" cooking experience. (That one is easy. This is it!)

They also asked me to send three (or more) of my favorite recipes. Now that's a tough one. I have a whole file box of recipes. Some of them I've clipped from *Grass and Grain* or somewhere. A lot of them, though, are my own. I'll try something occasionally that seems like a good idea. Some ideas are better than others. I'll have to sort through and decide which recipes to use for this project.

I've shared some of them with our five daughters, and they have their favorites. They think this is all pretty funny because Dad never cooked when they were growing up. Well, except for Thanksgiving turkey and dressing.

One of our favorite recipes is an outgrowth of the fact that we like breakfasts. Not necessarily in the morning, however. When we're traveling we'll sometimes stop at a truck stop or other eating place which serves breakfast 24 hours a day. They will know how to fix eggs, biscuits with sausage gravy, hash browns, all the rest. And their coffee will be good.

I noticed pretty quickly about when Edna would come home tired from a day herding second graders. One sure-fire way to cheer her up was a plate of sausage and eggs and hash browns with biscuits or toast.

That, in fact, is how I invented what is now one of our favorite one-dish meals: Start with a pound of bulk sausage, browned and drained. Cook a package of Ore-Ida Potatoes O'Brien according to directions, in a big skillet. Then stir in the sausage and a cup of grated cheddar cheese. Scoop out four "nests" in the potatoes and break an egg in each. Cover and cook a few minutes until the eggs are done to taste. Top with picante sauce to serve.

This recipe serves four, but it's easy to halve it for two people. It could be done with any other potatoes, but that particular style has onions and bell peppers already in it. That makes it fast and easy, which is one major requirement for anything I cook. Or for anyone, I guess, who operates on a tight schedule.

Maybe I should write a cookbook…At least, organize recipes.

See you down the road.

Animals and
Country Living

Lucky, A Horse January 1999

In 1971, when I started to write this weekly column, we were pretty active in the horse business. The editor of the old weekly *Emporia Times* had asked me to write a column about the 4H clubs with horse projects, and the area saddle clubs and their activities. That eventually evolved into this general interest, all-purpose column, so I hope I may be forgiven for reverting to one about a horse.

There's an old saying among cowboys that a man is allowed, in a lifetime, one good woman and one good horse. (I assume that similar is true for the cowgirls, but that isn't covered in the saying.) I have to say that as a family, we've been privileged to have several good horses. But the special one for me was undoubtedly a mare we called Lucky.

We were actively involved in breeding and showing Appaloosa horses. I was acting as a part-time breed inspector for the national organization. We wanted to expand our herd a little, and I was looking for a few young mares for breeding stock. I studied bloodlines extensively, rejected a couple of big name breeders because of what I considered poor breeding practices. We found ourselves in Nebraska, looking at some daughters of a national champion, Copper Dollar, one of the most versatile horses I ever saw. They used him to work cattle on the ranch, to ride for pleasure, and in performance competition, and he handled it all equally well.

We spent considerable time there, looking at Copper's foals, and checking their pedigrees. Finally, the owner said jokingly, "I'd sell you old Olive Oyl, there!" Olive was probably the ugliest mare I ever saw, but out of curiosity, I read her records. I was astonished. She had produced a number of highly superior foals, and their photographs showed a lot of what we wanted. One of her daughters had won the national champion trophy at halter as a two-year old. We finally bought a "four-horse package": Olive Oyl, her yearling colt, and her current year's foal. But what I really wanted was her unborn foal, sired by Copper Dollar and due the following January. A colt born early in the year has a big advantage in competition for the first couple of years.

That foal was born in our barn six months later, on January 13th, a Friday. What other name could she have but "Lucky"? It was a little bit disappointing that she was a nondescript mousy dun color. Appaloosas are *not* a color breed, but to show in breed competition, must be "recognizable." Lucky, as she matured, became a nice strawberry roan, and recognizable. She wasn't spectacular, but pretty predictable. Smooth...Not always first place, but always near the top. She did quite well, considering that on our Mid-American show circuit competition, we usually were competing against a couple of national champions. In open competition in 4H, Lucky had to compete against all breeds. We were laughed at by our quarter horse friends for our spotted horses, but the laughter changed in quality to some extent when Lucky began to win at performance. As far as I know, she's the only horse to win the performance trophy at the Lyon County Fair *twice*, against all comers. She had a shelf full of trophies and ribbons. Our daughter Connie, active in animal science studies at K-State, took her to Manhattan to participate in the horse activities there.

Lucky lost her eyesight as a fairly young mare, from an infection that struck our herd. But she adapted well, knew her way around the home pasture, and had meant a lot to all of us. She retired. I could relate a lot of other stories about her, but there isn't room. A horse is expected to live about twenty years. but Lucky just kept going. She left us last fall, on a warm sunny day in November. She'd have been thirty-two this month, over a hundred in human years. She rests, not a hundred yards from the barn where she was born. We'll surely miss her, but she didn't owe us a thing. She'd done it all.

See you down the road.

To Hypnotize a Chicken April 1999

I teach an adult Sunday school class, and have done so for thirty years. It's a pretty unorthodox group, and we often get far afield in the course of discussion. There's a lot of room for personal opinion, but no attempt to ridicule anybody or hurt anyone's feelings. I doubt that we've offended many, but there are other classes they could attend that are more conventional, if they prefer. All of this, to explain how we arrived, one Sunday, at the point of hypnotizing chickens.

We were discussing the description of Moses as he tries, in the book of Exodus, to convince the Pharaoh to let the Israelites leave. God has given him some miracles to demonstrate that the power is there. Specifically, Moses can cause his walking stick to turn into a snake. But Pharaoh's magicians and wise men demonstrate that *they* can do the same thing, and accuse him of a trick. Now I'm not questioning anyone's belief about how Moses did this, but how did *Pharaoh's* magicians manage to duplicate it?

I mentioned that somewhere I'd heard of a species of snake in that part of the world that can be hypnotized and stretched out perfectly straight. It would appear to be a walking stick. When it's tossed down on the ground, as Moses did, it would waken suddenly and become active, a snake again. Pharaoh's wise men would know about this, and use it to discredit Moses' demonstration if they could.

Other animals behave similarly in some circumstances as part of their adaptation for survival. Some respond to sounds, like the cobra in the snake charmer's basket. Consider the alligator, who is a dead log until the right moment, and then suddenly becomes a mouthful of teeth. The possum "plays possum" to pretend he's dead, and so does the American hog-nosed snake, who actually flops over on his back to play dead. (Turn him right side up, he'll turn back over, just to make sure you're convinced.)

In the course of all this, I mentioned to the class that hypnotizing that snake wouldn't be all that hard. Probably, not any tougher a job than hypnotizing a chicken. I got some very strange looks. Hypnotize a chicken? I was a little bit surprised that in that group, with a very broad range of experience, nobody seemed to know about chicken-hypnosis.

Until the present generation, every farm family and many families in town had a flock of laying hens to provide eggs. (I still think that a bowl of big brown-shelled eggs is much more appealing than today's mass-produced chalk-colored offering.) Of course, the kids in the family helped feed the chickens, and often played with them. Maybe, even took a young rooster over to the neighbors' for an impromptu cock-fight behind the barn when their mothers weren't watching.

But, back in my own childhood, my grandfather taught me how to calm a chicken so it was easier to handle. Birds are very much affected by light and darkness, he pointed out. Except for night birds, most consider darkness a cue to sleep. Some, he said, even sleep with their heads under their wings, to provide darkness. (I'm not sure about that one, but maybe…)

Anyway, he demonstrated for me that if you pick up a chicken and tuck its head under a wing, holding it in place, the bird will stop struggling and remain quiet. It was true. Motion, too, affects the bird's balance. He swung the chicken, head covered, in three moderately quick circles, and then released the head from under the wing. The bird stared, looking a bit confused and stupid. Well, sort of hypnotized. (Chickens often look confused and stupid, but this was a special case.)

Now he gently set the chicken on its feet, but with the tip of its beak on a chalk mark he'd made on the flagstone walk. It would stay that way until it thunders, Grandpa said. Well, it didn't. Something startled it in ten or fifteen minutes, and it retreated, cackling indignantly. All this is useful information, but actually it's pretty seldom that I'm called upon to hypnotize a chicken anymore.

See you down the road.

A Friendly Wave

When we first expanded our livestock operation to include a pasture north of town, I'm sure the neighbors up there were curious. They possibly suspected that it was some sort of tax shelter. (Actually, I have never had enough income to need much tax shelter.)

But I was driving an old station wagon. Our kids were small, and that's what we needed. It had a trailer hitch for the stock trailer and a two-horse rig that we used for 4-H and horse shows.

Finally there came a time when I realized, about 1970, that what we needed was a pickup truck. Pickups were not as common then. The drugstore cowboys hadn't discovered them yet. A pickup truck largely indicated that you were serious in intent.

I found a used half-ton Chevy which proved to be just what was needed. I could load 52 small square bales of hay on it, with practice. Of course, that was three or four times the weight it was designed for, but for short distances, necessity...well, you know.

There was another side effect of driving that old pickup. The neighbors, who had by now been waving as they recognized me, now waved in a slightly different manner. I felt accepted. This was especially true if another factor or two were in evidence. 1) A load of hay, or a spool of wire and some posts. Or 2) If I was wearing my cowboyin' hat.

In those cases, I'd get an even friendlier wave. Not just from people who recognized me, but from anybody in a pickup truck who was wearing a big hat. It was an open-handed, friendly wave, palm forward, a universal greeting in friendship in all cultures, maybe Brotherhood (or Sisterhood, of course).

The hat part is interesting. When I was a kid, you could often tell a person's occupation by his hat. It was sort of a trademark. It marked him as a rancher (different from a farmer, but also marked by his footwear). Bankers, business men, and railroaders could also be identified by their hats. Clergymen in some cases wore a clerical collar (or had their shirts on backward, I was never certain).

Now, almost everyone wears a baseball cap, which may indicate how the whole world is going to hell in a handbasket. It's hard to spot a cowboy in a baseball cap. Besides, he gets his ears sunburned. I even heard of a cowboy who was wearing tennis shoes instead of boots so folks wouldn't think he was a truck driver.

Back to the friendly wave...I heard a speaker not long ago who was stating that the wave is regional. A broad, open-palm wave in our part of the state. But in other areas, the flatlands in particular, it's different. Drivers of pickups still wave, but in a really flat part of the country, such as western Kansas, there isn't a need for a broad wave, he said. There's not a lot else in sight, so a simpler motion will suffice.

That speaker demonstrated. He held both hands in front of him as if they were at the top of a steering wheel. Then for the greeting he merely straightened his index finger, pointing upward for about two seconds. Then, back around the wheel with the others.

I was on a long trip to western Kansas recently, driving my pickup (Not the 1968 model, however.) I determined a trio of facts.

1) People driving pickup trucks do still wave at people driving pickup trucks.
2) The wave is more enthusiastic if you're wearing a broad-brimmed hat.
3) They really do use the index-finger wave out there. I found that I could do it myself, and pass for a native.

The speaker from whom I heard that theory had suggested another. Different sorts of greetings could be expressed, he said, by the use of other fingers. I did not test that theory.

See you down the road.

A Matter of Survival August 2001

A few years ago there was a ripple of interest in the fact that house plants do better if you talk to them gently. Mostly, it was considered a joke, but there were a few actual experiments, with measurable results. Soft music, gentle conversation and loving words seemed to cause plants to thrive. Conversely, those exposed to hard rock "music" did poorly, much like humans in similar situations. This quite possibly accounts for the "green thumb" phenomena. Some people are skilled at caring for plants. Anything they try will grow. Others can kill the healthiest plant very quickly, with about the same degree of care.

There are exceptions to this rule. We knew a lady who became disgusted with a non-performing gardenia, and had a talk with it. Actually, she cussed the wretched thing, called it vile names, and threatened to toss it in the trash can. At least, that was her story. I wasn't present at the cussing, but I did see the plant covered with glorious bloom a few weeks later. And, this woman has certainly never claimed to have a green thumb.

That led me to a story about an eccentric orchardist who, disgusted with a few of his poorly-performing trees, took an axe out to the orchard. He'd explain to each tree that those who don't produce were to become firewood. Then he'd whack the trunk three or four times with the back of the axe head. The next season produced a bumper crop of apples.

It wasn't long after that when I heard of a strange custom among some of the fruit growers in California. It may come from the Mediterranean, I understand. At a certain time of the year, they have a ritual talk with each tree, and beat the trunk with a padded club or rolled-up newspaper. This "wakes" the tree and starts the sap to flowing, I'm told.

What do all these things have in common? It would seem to hint that the plant perceives a threat to its existence. How? I don't know. But plants do respond to their environment. A vine reaches for something on which to climb. Where does *conscious* effort begin? Maybe it's only a matter of time until somebody organizes a battalion of well-meaning and well-funded nut-cases to carry placards demanding Plants' Rights. (And I may be sorry I suggested that.)

Reduced to the simplest terms, this is probably a lesson in survival of the fittest. There's a built-in urge to survive and perpetuate the species, in any living thing. In changing climates and conditions, a threat to any species brings out the same reaction: Become prolific. The bloom, and the production of fruit reflect this. It has shown itself in the past year. The summer of 2000 was hot and dry, followed by the coldest winter in a decade. Many trees and landscaping plants died or were severely damaged. But the flowering trees and shrubs which survived put on a marvelous show in the spring of 2001. It wasn't all good. Drains and gutters were clogged with the bumper crop of seeds from elms and soft maples. On the other hand, many farmers had a heavy yield from winter wheat. Better than expected.

Two years ago I noticed a seedling soft maple tree near the stock tank in the pasture at home. It wasn't in a bad place, was about eight feet tall, and was growing well, so I decided to leave it. But there was a weak fork, about five feet from the ground. It would never do. I could cut out one side, but then the tree would be tall and spindly...I decided to "girdle" the unwanted branch, but leave it on the tree for a season, as a support for the other fork. I stripped the bark from the appropriate fork in a four-inch strip and tied the "good" branch to it. I'd cut the dead branch away at the end of the season.

Except, the girdled branch didn't die. It never even wilted. Through the hot summer...The branch was apparently drawing water up through the dry and brittle girdled stem, acting as a wick. Well, it would never survive a winter. But it did. When spring came, both sides of the tree came to life. An odd thing, though. The two branches of that fork bore no resemblance at all. The "good" side was growing vigorously, leaves and new stems and branches, but not one bloom. The girdled branch was very scarce on leaves, but heavy with bloom, and eventually with seed. How did it know?

See you down the road.

Back to Basics

We've had a pretty serious stretch of winter this year, a great deal of it before winter actually began. I have no way of knowing what the weather might be doing by the time you read this. That's some time ahead, and with the weather as unpredictable as it has been for the past season or two, who knows? Several all-time low temperatures have been recorded, despite "global warming" theories.

On a more pragmatic level, such weather does create different problems for people with livestock. They require more attention and more care. Taking care of our cow-calf herd is my exercise. A writer has to do something physical after a few hours of sitting. Some might play racquet ball or jog to exercise, but the folks who jog past our house never look like they're having very much fun. I'd rather water cows, fix fence and haul feed. I get to observe nature, "write" in my head, get some fresh air and exercise, and be productive at the same time. We'll market several tons of beef "on the hoof" this year, as we always do.

In weather like we've had, the effort becomes a bit more intensive, of course. There are a few other factors, too. I've seen more coyotes. Coyotes' numbers wax and wane, but several ranchers up in the north end of the county tell me they've seen more. The Extension Service recently had a program on K-State radio dealing with coyote "predation." (Now there's a good word.) Newborn calves are pretty vulnerable to a family of predatory coyotes. We haven't had much trouble. It may be because we have an aged, retired donkey in the same pasture. Donkeys apparently have an instinct about predators. I've seen them attack dogs, and once found a young coyote in our pasture behind the house that appeared to have been trampled to death. There were several horses in that pasture...And, the one old donkey. I'd bet on the donkey.

Through the years, we've had more trouble with feral dogs. "Feral" is another good word, meaning domestic animals that have reverted to the wild. Sometimes, even, a pack of dogs that may have started with animals that have been "dumped" may be joined by others that really belong to somebody. This could lead to a potentially dangerous situation, since such dogs would have very little fear of humans. I know of several incidents over the years. Usually they're handled by the ranchers whose livelihood is being threatened, as they defend their herds and flocks.

In recent years, there has been a constant push by well-meaning people who really aren't involved, to "re-introduce" various predators into some areas. The main argument is usually that they were there at one time...Restore grizzly bears to Colorado, it has been recently suggested. They were there once. Wolves, to Yellowstone Park. That's being tried, with a variety of results. There are two major problems: One is that most predators don't read boundary markers, and find neighboring calves and sheep easier prey than elk and buffalo. The other is that such "restoration" projects are usually initiated by well-meaning, well-funded animal lovers who have no expertise in wildlife management. It should be left to the trained specialists, who unfortunately are subject to political pressure via their funding.

This sometimes results in some pretty bizarre situations. A few decades ago there were congressional hearings about a problem with coyotes in the sheep country in Colorado, Wyoming, and Utah. These are big areas, far from civilization. Coyote control has ranged from shooting, trapping, and poisoning to bounties paid by the states for coyote scalps. (Kansas had coyote bounties not many years ago.)

The hearings had been initiated by city-dwelling "environmentalists" who were shocked at the cruelty of controlling coyote predation by getting rid of coyotes. There was actually a suggestion that instead of killing the offending predators, they should be neutered to prevent coyote overpopulation, which they saw as the problem. This might be done biologically, they argued, by putting out bait laced with birth-control pills.

This was too much for one old sheep rancher from up on Green River.

"You people don't understand!" he sputtered. "The coyotes are not *breeding* our sheep, they are *eating* them!"

See you down the road.

Mama Was A Pickup Truck   September 2001

Back when our kids were small, we had a few half-wild bantam chickens around the barn. They were fun to watch, and they'd hide out their nests in the brush and around our old outbuildings. In the course of things, I decided that it would be educational to incubate a couple of eggs under a light bulb, so that the kids could watch the hatching process. We turned the eggs by hand faithfully, and lo and behold, one actually hatched...A cute, fluffy black chick. The girls named it "George," for no apparent reason.

George turned out to be a female, and she had all the maternal instincts built in. When she matured, she knew all about finding a place for her *own* nest, "setting" for the prescribed three weeks, and mothering a brood of chicks. Her DNA carried an instinct that told her what to do. George was a good mother, despite the fact that until she was grown she had never even *seen* a mother hen. She raised several broods of chicks.

***

All of this came back to mind in the last year or so. I wrote about a January Sunday in 1999, when I found one of our cows with twin calves. I spent most of the day driving around our pasture in the pickup, with one of the calves in the front seat. The mother had accepted the other twin, but refused this one. (Not uncommon, I understand.) Finally, I had to resort to taking the rejected twin home to raise on a bottle. A couple of our girls, home for a visit, named her "Monica." (Don't ask.)

Monica grew up, looking exactly like her twin. I couldn't tell them apart now without reading their brands. Both were pretty good females, and I wondered if they might also "twin," so I kept them as replacements, out of curiosity.

I was in for some surprises. First, you have to understand that the main part of our cow-calf operation is a few miles north of the home place. Usually, I have a few replacement calves at home, but that season I had none, by sheer coincidence. Monica had grown up around barn cats. I had noticed her odd behavior around the riding lawn mower, following it closely along the other side of the fence. This was curious, and somewhat puzzling. I didn't tumble to the reason until she was grown and I took her out to the pasture and turned her in with the other cows. She had never seen another cow, except for the first few hours of her life, when she was being kicked in the face by her mother. She kept trying to follow me back to the truck. Finally the herd wandered off, leaving her to stand watching in bewilderment. It eventually soaked into my head...Newborn bonding! She doesn't know she's a cow. She thinks the red truck is her mama...The lawn mower, also red, must be her little brother. At least, I figured that she thought so.

It took several weeks for Monica to decide that she was one of those four-legged critters, and belonged with the bunch. Now, she's perfectly happy with them, but still comes over to visit with the pickup truck when I drive into the pasture.

All of that, of course, was nearly two years ago. This past spring, I was eager to see how the calving would go. I was expecting a calf from both of the twins. There is a condition in which, when a cow carries twins of opposite sexes, the female will be sterile. (This is called a "freemartin," and I have no idea why.) But that would not apply here, since both twins are female. But would *they* be likely to have twins?

The other twin delivered first, a nice bull calf, with no problems. It was three weeks later that Monica calved, the time difference probably marking the disadvantage of not having a mama to furnish all her needs. But her calf was a nice heifer...(Really nice. I may keep her for a replacement.)

Now that calf may have a red Chevy pickup for a grandma, but the mother instinct came through again. Monica's inborn mothering instinct is intact. In spite of the fact that she had never seen a mother cow, except for one that kept kicking her in the face, she knows everything that a cow is suppose to know about taking care of a baby calf. She's one of the best mamas we've ever had.

See you down the road.

Tick Fever

At this time of the year, more people are spending more time out-doors. That's a good thing, because fresh air and sunshine are healthy. I'm more oriented to outdoor activities that bring people into contact with nature's wonders than to sports events, because I think they learn more. At least, some do. Some philosopher whose wisdom I once read is quoted as having said something like "God does not deduct from man's allotted time on earth those hours spent in fishing." I suppose that goes for women fishermen too, and for those who just like to spend some time on the top of a hill watching the wind blow across the tallgrass prairie.

That's the good part. The other side of the story involves some of the less pleasant aspects, such as sunburn, chiggers, mosquitoes, and ticks. We know a lot more, in the past few decades, about the dangers of sun on skin, and why Arabs wear so many clothes. Of the insect hazards, most of them in our part of the country are primarily a nui-sance rather than a hazard. We can use insect repellents, and a bit of common sense, both of which are a help.

The critters that really alarm people most often, though, are ticks. Mention these bugs, and watch facial expressions. (Ugh!) Granted, ticks can carry disease. Currently the greatest fear is Lyme disease. Before that, spotted fever. During the great cattle drives of a century ago, many herds were quarantined because of disease-carrying ticks. There are a lot of wild tales, bordering on superstition, about the almost supernatural qualities of the creatures. Also, a myriad of theories about the best way to remove ticks.

I was once told that if you have any task with several different ways that it can be accomplished, you can count on one thing: "None of them are worth a damn." If any of the methods worked well, there would be no others. This holds true on removal of ticks.

Now to back up just a little, I have had a lifelong association with ticks. As a kid on the farm of an aunt and uncle, as a Boy Scout, work-ing as a surveyor's "chainman," working at a youth camp, in mountain artillery with Army mules, as a YMCA director in outdoor recreation, with our own kids on the ranch, with a variety of livestock, and for years as a physician.

I have removed ticks from cats, dogs, chickens, horses, mules, guineas, cattle, rabbits, campers, soldiers, friends, a spouse, our own offspring, and medical patients. I have tried every suggestion I ever heard of for easy tick removal: Turpentine, kerosene, gasoline, whiskey, ice, a hot coal, on and on. There are better uses for most of the products mentioned, and a couple are getting too expensive to try. All worked equally well…That is, very seldom. The usual sequence was always the same: 99% of the time, every method failed. Usually it killed the tick, so he couldn't turn loose. I once actually read in a reputable medical journal that it required a "gentle counterclockwise twist" to remove the tick. This is based on the old superstition that the tick's nose is equipped with a screw thread, which must be *unscrewed* to remove. (But what if you chanced on a tick with a left-hand thread?) This didn't really work either. Practically always, I had to revert to Plan B, in which there are two steps: **1)** Grasp the tick, and **2)** Pull it off with a quick jerk. A small patch of superficial skin cells comes with it.

But, some quick jerk is bound to protest: There's a risk of leaving the head or "mouth parts" embedded. First, among the hundreds or maybe thousands of ticks that I've removed, I know of that happening only once. It was in the belly button of a camp counselor. It "festered out," which is nature's way of removing small foreign bodies from superficial skin scrapes and scratches anyway.

What about more serious infections, such as spotted fever or Lyme disease? Of course, there's a risk, but rarely a major risk. There's a risk to living. We might be hit by a truck or struck by lightning. Spotted fever has a trademark: Red-spotted palms on the hands, spots the size of a pinhead. Lyme disease is characterized by a "target" rash: A bullseye at the point of the bite, and a red ring around it. Both diseases are treatable with antibiotics. If in doubt, see a doctor.

See you down the road.

Old Cowboy

Lyon County lost another of our old cowboys last month when Lee Bryant crossed over.

I didn't know Lee as well as I have some of the others, but I always enjoyed talking to him. I've always felt that I'd like to know him better. Here was a man who really knew cattle and Flint Hills rangeland. He was low-key, with marvelous powers of observation and quiet good humor.

Two episodes come to mind when I think about Lee. Oddly, both are associated with fishing. He used to go out with a mutual friend to fish in one of our pasture ponds.

Unknown to either of them, I'd had trouble with a couple of old cows. They had learned to hook a horn under a wire on the fence and with a quick jerk, pop a staple loose. Then pretty quickly the whole herd would be out in the road, in my neighbor's wheat or in somebody else's pasture. As a temporary measure, I had rigged a particularly weak section of fence with an extra, battery-driven electric wire to keep the cattle off of it. I'd either do a better repair or take the escape artist to the sale later.

Neither of the fishermen knew about this hot wire, and the box was across the little creek and behind a tree. They divided forces to crawl through the fence, and Lee, on the east side of the creek, selected the section with the juiced wire. History does not record what he said when he discovered it, but his fishing partner thought it was pretty funny. I never had the nerve to ask Lee about it.

The other event involved another fishing trip and an old cow of mine. She was getting close to voting age when she developed a bad problem with her udder. She had lost her calf that spring, probably because it was unable to nurse. I knew that another calf would have the same tragic end. There comes a time when even a good old cow has to go. It's both a financial burden and a humane thing.

I watched the sale, and prices were high. (It goes without saying that this was some years ago.) After my cattle sold and I watched a little while, I headed down toward the office to pick up my check. In the hall, I encountered Lee Bryant.

"Well," he greeted, "were you happy with what that old white-faced cow brought?"

I admitted that I was, and that I was a bit surprised that prices were so good to the seller.

"Sometimes you just hit it right," he observed. "I knew you'd be bringin' her in, though. I told Joe when we were out there fishin', you'd have to cull her this year."

I was astonished. I knew that the last time those guys had been out to our pond was at least five weeks before. Lee, who wasn't even out there to look at cattle, had picked the one with the problem out of a herd of thirty or so. Then he'd been at the sale barn and at other places where he'd looked at cows ever since.

He'd actually looked at several thousand cattle in the intervening weeks. Yet, when my old cow came through the sale ring, Lee not only recognized her, but her problem, where he'd seen her before, and the circumstances. And this was just a white-faced cow, looking a lot like several hundred others going through the sale ring that day. I can't even remember that well, the *people* I meet. It was a special example of an old cowboy's expertise.

Once in a while a non-livestock person will ask how we tell our cows apart. Well, they look different, just as people do. But once in a while comes a man like Lee Bryant, who could pick my old cow out of the thousands he'd seen since, and remember her.

There was a real cowboy.

See you down the road.

A Labor of Love July 1995

A few years ago I was recounting to a friend some misadventure with livestock, and he asked me a question which really made me stop and think.

"Why do you do it?"

He went on to point out that I had responsibilities to take care of horses and cattle in all kinds of weather. Wet, dry, freezing and burning heat. Large animals can also step on your feet, crowd you into a fence, give you all sorts of problems. They sometimes sicken and die, with considerable financial loss. Even at best, the market is unpredictable, and a year's hard work may result in very little gain.

I couldn't very well explain to him, and this made me wonder if I could explain it to myself. Ours has never been a very big operation. We raise no more than twenty-five or thirty calves in any year, and we have other occupations, too. But the livestock business has always been important to us.

I recalled a remark of Baxter Black's. He'd never seen a cowboy, he said, who was saving up money to buy into a hardware store. However, he knew a lot of cowboys who were working in a hardware store or some such job, trying to save up to get back in the cattle business. Now why is this?

I tried to explain to my friend that it was for the exercise. Some people jog, or walk or run, play tennis or golf. But none of these really appeal to me. The runners and joggers who go past our place don't appear to be having a great deal of fun.

Golfers deserve special comment. There are a lot of golf jokes, which are really too easy. But something that's done for the exercise? Golf involves riding in a cart to where you get out, whack a little ball a couple of hundred yards, ride to that spot and whack it again. Even the equipment used is carried by someone else or in the cart. Well, to each his own. It's a way to get outdoors, and to do gender things.

But back to my story…In the end, the exercise excuse for raising cattle and horses seemed pretty lame, even to me. So, why *do* we do it? I still didn't know.

About that time we were trying to upgrade the cow herd by artificial breeding. One of our daughters took the course at Kansas State University, and came home to teach me. This involved frozen semen and a tank of liquid nitrogen, and working out a routine suitable for our operation. Connie and I worked together on it, and had a certain amount of success.

That particular summer, she had gone on to other occupations. I was using a schedule that coordinated the fertility cycles of the cows, but required intensive observation. Specifically, I'd watch the animals for a half hour at dawn and again at dusk for ten consecutive days. It was hot weather but both times were not at all unpleasant.

Each morning as I'd sit watching for activity, I'd notice an older man in a pickup truck with a bale spike in the back. He'd drive past on the road and we'd wave. He would go somewhere, pick up a single big bale of prairie hay on the spike, and wave on his way back. I didn't know who he was, where he was getting the hay, or where he took it every morning.

One morning my cows were grazing near the road. Instead of driving the extra half mile to the pasture gate and back, I parked on the road and sat on the hood of the pickup. The old man drove past on schedule and we waved. But on his way back he stopped, parked behind me, and came over to visit. We remarked on the beautiful morning, and he made a couple of observations about my cattle.

Then he asked a question that wasn't really a question: "Don't you feel sorry for folks that live in town and don't get to do things like this?"

That was it, I realized. We both were out there, doing jobs that we could have gotten somebody else to do. But then, we'd be missing out on the fun of it. We wouldn't have the excuse to get out at dawn and enjoy the cool beauty of a summer sunrise. We do it because we love it.

See you down the road.

The Blue Hen's Chick

December 1998

A few weeks ago the Emporia *Gazette* ran a series of articles about cockfighting. It was a front-page series, and drew a lot of attention, with a wide range of emotions. I had a couple of phone calls suggesting that I enter the discussion with a column on the subject. I refused at first, on the basis that my columns are written four to six weeks in advance, and it would be old news. Also, it's not a local column, and would be of little interest to most of the communities whose newspapers carry the column. Gradually, I began to see that maybe it would make a viable topic.

One of the precipitating factors in the *Gazette's* series was a change in city ordinances a couple of years ago, prohibiting the keeping of chickens within the city limits. I suppose the time comes when every town has to face this problem. Until a generation ago, many families in town kept a few hens to furnish eggs. It seemed logical. We're not in the city yet, and have livestock, but until a few years ago we also had chickens. Some of our kids made their spending money selling eggs.

But what *kind* of chickens? To a lot of people, apparently, a chicken is a chicken. Not really, any more than a dog is just a dog. In both species, there are dozens of special-purpose breeds. There are heavy breeds of chickens for meat, Mediterranean types for egg producers, and miniature bantams for hobby or show. There are even highly specialized Japanese types bred solely for their tail feathers, which may be several feet long. Those iridescent black feathers are used in traditional costuming, hats, and art objects. And of course, there are game chickens. Quite a few fighting gamecocks are raised in Kansas. Nothing illegal about it, as long as they don't *fight* in Kansas. But to raise fighting chickens, it requires that one have quite a few roosters on hand at any given time. Roosters are noted for crowing, and this became part of Emporia's problem.

After the city ordinance was enacted to remove them from town, there were actually complaints from some *country* neighbors about crowing roosters. I found that a bit ludicrous. To me, a part of country life had always been the crowing of roosters. It's a pastoral sound, reassuring that all's well with the world, and of considerably more comfort than sirens and traffic noise. This is another example of a strange phenomenon in our society. People see a wonderful place, which inspires them to move there. Yet, once there, they can't wait to destroy the very things that made them love it, and recreate it to look exactly like where they came from.

But, back to cockfighting. No matter how distasteful many find it, the sport is deep-seated in our culture. It's still legal in several states, and there are many signs that indicate that cockfighting was once not only acceptable, but economically important. One of Emporia's best Mexican restaurants is called *El Palenque*, the "cockpit," the arena where the cockfight takes place. The term in aviation for the most important area of activity is, of course, the cockpit, named after the fighting cockpit.

The state bird of Delaware is a game cock, the Blue Hen's Chick. This requires a little explanation. Traditionally, at least in that area, the best fighting cocks were hatched from eggs laid by a blue hen. That they'd choose the "blue hen's chick" as the state bird indicates remarkable knowledge and acceptance of the sport.

"Sport?" Here we come to the main point of the whole thing. Since humans first domesticated other creatures, they have enjoyed watching them. Peacocks strut, birds sing, dogs hunt, horses run and jump. Animals follow their instincts, and are interesting to observe. Many of these instincts involve fighting, and special strains are created by selective breeding, to bring out aggressive tendencies. Thus, we have cattle to participate in bullfights, pit bull dogs for fighting in an arena, even Siamese fighting fish. Gamecocks fight. Even men try to batter each other into unconsciousness in the boxing ring. Where do we draw the line? Somewhere, fun becomes cruelty. It's just a matter of where.

So, a chicken isn't just a chicken. Interesting, though, that the logo bird on the *Gazette's* cockfighting series wasn't a fighting gamecock, but an "ornamental" breed, a show type bantam.

See you down the road.

On Thin Ice
April 1995

As I'm writing this, there's snow on the ground. We've seen snow here in April, but it's still March, and March is a slob. It's also calving time and the old joke that the heifers will wait for a good blizzard to calve isn't very funny.

We had that winter storm, the second week in March, and calves were popping out all over. It was going pretty well, no major problems. It helps maybe, that they're born with a fur coat. We had about a dozen on the ground, and more on the way, when we got a nice sunny day for a change. Sunshine on the backs of livestock is a wonderful remedy for anything, even with snow underfoot.

I spent a little while counting cows and calves, and could pretty well account for everybody. Then, an hour or so moving big bales with the tractor, so they'd have something to eat. Fill water tanks, usual winter chores. It was going well, and the temperature was almost up to freezing.

There were a couple of minor maintenance jobs on the tractor. There always are, I guess. I accomplished those, put fresh gas in it for next time, and got in the pickup to go home. One last glance around the pasture...

Down by the pond were three cows with new calves. One mama was pacing along the bank looking worried. There on the ice was her new calf, slipping and sliding and trying to get up.

Remember in the movie Bambi, the fawn slipping and sliding on ice? It was exactly like that, except not nearly so amusing. This was the deepest part of the pond, the steepest bank on the pond dam. The ice was thin...Not more than an inch or two, and with the warm sun, it was pretty rotten ice. A very dangerous situation. Every time the calf struggled to his feet he'd slip and fall again. To make matters worse, he was sliding farther out onto the pond. He knew which way to go, but couldn't get any traction. Like the story of the frog in the well, who could jump two feet up, but only by sliding back three.

I turned to the pickup to get a rope. I always carry a lariat, for such emergencies. But I'd cleaned out the pickup a while back, and it wasn't there. (A message, maybe, that pickup trucks should not be cleaned out.) I rummaged a little in the tool box, but no rope. I'd known that.

I drove to my neighbor's house a mile and a half away, and there was no one home. I didn't feel like looking around his barn for a rope. His dog might not appreciate it, either.

I started back to the pond, wondering if I could twist enough baling wire together to reach the calf. If not…I hated to think about it. About a half mile down the road, I met my neighbor in his truck, flagged him down, and quickly explained.

While he went for a lariat, I put out a sack of range cubes to decoy the rest of the herd out and away from the problem. One or two mama cows stayed with the pair in trouble as a sort of support group. Mothers understand these things.

When we got down to the pond, the calf had slid farther out on the ice. The rope was pretty short, but could be made to reach. We couldn't get any closer. As it was, we were breaking through the crusty ice at the edge and sinking through into mud.

It took about five throws to get a loop over the calf, and we didn't have a foot of rope to spare. Now, if he'd just hold still and not shake the loop off…Even drawing it tight was an edgy chore.

All this time, Mama was pacing the top of the dam above us, talking to the calf, and acting very nervous. As well she might, of course. But there was the possibility that she might blame *us* for her baby's problems and come storming down the slope, too.

Finally, we got the rope snug, slid the calf across the ice and shoved him up the slope to mama. They both trotted off.

"Well, Don," said my neighbor, "sometimes it comes out right."

See you down the road.

The New Pickup

When I'm out around the state I meet a lot of people. Many of them tell me stories, which is great, because that's my thing. No writer could make up stuff like that which really happens. Especially, I think, to people who are in the livestock business, in farming, or who have kids. Or, of course, all of the above. Teachers deal with kids, too, and have some pretty good stories.

So, I pick up stories everywhere. I can't honestly recall where I heard this one. I jotted some notes, set them aside, and they surfaced again recently. So, whoever gave this one, thanks!

The family had just bought a brand new pickup, which is always a really exciting time. There is a period when it stands gleaming and pristine, and a source of pride for the whole family. It's kept clean and uncluttered, even, for a little while. At least until the first scratch or ding.

Now any farm or ranch pickup is going to receive that first damage. It may be years before the next, or may not, but it's the *first* one that we remember. Sort of like the first scuff on a pair of new boots.

In this case, however, it was more than a scuff. It happened only days after they brought the pickup home. They were working cattle, and an old cow decided that the source of all her problems was that shiny new monster over there. She did an effective job on one of the doors. Not quite enough to total the door, apparently, though maybe so. (I'm not sure of my notes, here.)

In any case, the new or repaired and straightened door had to be repainted. Once again, the new pickup sat gleaming with pride out by the barn.

But there are apparently mysterious qualities about automotive paints and finishes. For one thing, they attract runaway shopping carts. There's another factor there, too, a time factor. This attractive force begins to fade in a year or so. (Did you ever see a shopping cart hit an *old* car?)

Brand new paint on a vehicle, though, possesses the most powerful of attractive forces. Apparently, not only to shopping carts, but to horses. The family in this story looked over at the renovated pickup to see one of their horses calmly chewing off the new paint.

It recalled to me an incident a lot of years ago when we first moved into our present home. The pond up behind the house had some pretty good bass, and a friend asked to bring his kids out to do a little fishing. I wouldn't be home, but that was okay, I told him.

That pond is only a stone's throw from the house, and I assumed that he'd park in the yard and walk up there. Instead he drove through the gate and parked at the pond. That was okay, of course. He'd shut the gate like a responsible guest.

A little later, as they were fishing, he glanced up to see a couple of our horses happily chewing the paint off the trunk of his new Cadillac. (I've never really understood why his fishing car was his new caddy, though.)

In my limited research on the subject, however, I have developed the theory that new automotive finishes attract not only shopping carts and horses, but buffalo. Some friends, a number of years ago, bought a young buffalo heifer, and turned her out with their cattle.

When "Rosalie" delivered her first crossbred calf, they were understandably eager to see it. They drove out into the pasture in their brand new pickup. It was not a good move.

We saw the remains a couple of days later. When a buffalo and a pickup truck disagree, the pickup is the loser. At least, based on that incident. The vehicle was all but totaled. Both headlights, the grill, dents along the body...Major dents...Radiator punctured and drained. Apparently they had been fortunate just to be able to drive it back to the house.

No one was hurt, and they gained a healthy respect for Rosalie's right to raise her calf in any way she saw fit. She did produce many more, over the years, but the pickup was not so lucky.

See you down the road.

A Woman and a Horse

We had an interesting house guest last month, a niece from Houston. My wife's niece, actually, though she's *our* niece now.

Kaaren is in her forties, looks much younger, and on this visit looked wonderfully trim and healthy. The reason, she explained, is a horse. She's lost a few pounds, and was vibrant and excited as she whipped out a handful of photos like a new grandmother who's a fast-draw artist. But let's back up a ways...

This young woman has not had the easiest life. She married young, had one child, and in a few years, a divorce. She's a self-propelled unit, however, somewhat of a "feminist" in the best sense of the expression. With her natural initiative, her computer skills and some experience in accounting, she set up her own home-based company. She can do anything from monthly payroll to total bookkeeping for a corporation to somebody's income taxes, and everything beyond and between. She still runs the business out of her house, and has one virtually full time employee.

Her son is grown now, and after some rough times is employed and doing well. She has dated, but never remarried. She has had a wide range of interests and some interesting friends, but I've always felt that she likes to come to our place to let her hair down. She goes out with me to feed cattle, and loves to just sit on our back porch and watch the horses in the pasture. Her dream has always been the "quiet place in the country," I guess.

Kaaren has always driven flashy little sports cars of one kind or other. (She's probably a little bit "lead-footed," like some of the other female members of that branch of the family.) She understands cars and driving. It was a bit of a shock, then, to see her tool into our driveway this time behind the wheel of a white extended-cab Chevy pickup truck.

Well, we knew that she had a horse. She had called last fall to ask advice about it. But, we had no idea that it had gone this far. She was wearing jeans and well-worn boots and would have fit right in at any rodeo. Gradually, with the aid of her quick-draw photos, we became acquainted with Buck, her horse, and saw pictures of trail rides, parades, and rodeos.

She had had a friend who owned a horse. Kaaren had been out to the stable a few times, and had become interested in what was going on, in the people and the horses. She began to think about buying a horse, so she could ride when she wanted. For some reason her friend resented this interest, and tried in every way to discourage it. That woman is now referred to as "my former friend."

But there were other horse people around, who assisted, encouraged, advised and eventually helped her find and buy "Buck." It's probably the best thing that ever happened to Kaaren.

She rides every weekend now, and has a whole new set of friends. Better friends, she says, than the crowd she used to run with. (Well, these are horse people.) The partner with whom she rides is a retired individual named Jim, a former saddlemaker, tack salesman and frustrated cowboy. His 21-year old horse, Hobo, was saved from becoming dog food when Jim came along. That's another story, of course.

It became apparent that Buck would need to be transported sometimes to trail rides, rodeos, etc. The solution? Buy a trailer, of course. The Chevy pickup pulls it well, and now she occasionally contracts to haul horses for other people. Once, as far as Dallas, to deliver an animal for a friend.

I've seen an interest in horses making a difference in peoples' lives before, but rarely to this extent. This young woman is healthy, happy, and having *fun*. She looks and feels like a horseman (horseperson?) because she *is*. And in a way she does have her place in the country, because she can "hang out at the barn" with people of similar interest. And the bumper sticker on the white pickup says *"A Woman's Place is On A Horse."*

See you down the road.

A Herd of Turkeys

May 1994

In the middle 1930's, we had some really strange weather in Kansas. I was at a very impressionable age then, and I well remember the dust storms which made it hard to breathe. My mother tied wet cloths over the faces of her family, and in a short while the areas over mouth and nose would be black with mud from the dust that was filtered out by breathing. It would be twilight at noon, and you couldn't see a street light from a block away. It was pretty scary.

We had an aunt and uncle on a farm about twenty miles away, and I spent a lot of time there during those summers. I'm not sure of the year, but for two or three of those dreadfully different summers they had a plague of grasshoppers. The insects numbered in the millions, and were pretty destructive. I can recall corn fields stripped down to stubble, peach trees with no more leaves than they'd had in December. Fruit was one of the more important Kansas crops then, before wheat came to its peak later. It must have been devastating to a farmer to watch grasshoppers destroy his orchard before his very eyes. There were stories of grasshoppers chewing on the skin of infants in cribs, leaving raw patches.

In a more jocular vein, jokes of exaggeration sprang up to relieve the tragic tension. There was the man hoeing corn who, when the swarm settled, had the straw hat eaten from his head and the wooden handle of his hoe eaten in two as he ran for shelter. In another variation, an ax handle at the chopping block by the kitchen door was eaten, leaving only the metal head of the ax stuck in the block. (I wondered why they didn't eat the chopping block, too. Well, it's a story.)

All of this was recalled not long ago when I saw a reference to the grasshopper plagues in a magazine article. It involved Dr. Arthur Hertzler, the famous Kansas "horse and buggy doctor" who founded the well-known clinic at Halstead.

Dr. Hertzler was an innovator, not only in medicine but in any field which caught his attention. He tried various financial endeavors, and was apparently moderately successful at most of them.

The grasshopper connection occurred when Dr. Hertzler had an idea about how to use the insects rather than fight them. He bought several hundred young turkeys, called "poults." After a reasonable start in a poultry shed, he would turn the birds out to be "herded" like sheep or cattle. The herdsman were teenage boys, hired for the summer job of turkey-herding. Each was armed with a long bamboo fishing pole, a red bandana tied on the tip. The boys would turn out the herd each morning and drive the birds out into grasshopper-infested open country.

There was apparently a standard route which they followed, a big loop at a quiet pace that took all day. Any strays were encouraged back into the flock by the flags on the long cane poles. It apparently worked relatively well, because grasshoppers were in abundance, fattening the birds by the end of the summer.

That's a great example of an idea that would work one time, in a special circumstance, and maybe never again. Probably there were a lot of people who asked themselves "why didn't I think of that?" Or, who thought it was a great idea when they heard of it later. It takes a special genius to see an idea and act on it, in time to make good. Dr. Hertzler was one of those people.

This recalled a similar story from the era of the "great buffalo hunts" in the 1870's. An entrepreneur in Tulsa saw that the animals were being slaughtered by the thousands for only the tongue or the hide. The rest was left to rot.

His idea was to take advantage of the situation. He bought several hundred young hogs in Tulsa, and hired a crew to herd them out onto the prairie. For all summer they followed the hunts, moving in behind the skinners to allow the herd to feed on the abundant repast scattered across the plains.

At the season's end they drove the now-fattened butcher pigs back to the stockyards to sell. Of course, either of these men could have lost his shirt. But they didn't.

See you down the road.

The Nokota Horses

May 1994

I mentioned earlier this month our experiences at the Iowa Horse Fair. One of the highlights for me was to become acquainted with a unique breed of horse, the Nokota Horse. There has been an established registry for the breed only since 1991, but their history is fascinating.

The American Indians saw their first horses with the coming of the Spanish, beginning in the 1500's in the south, and the early 1700's in the northern states and Canada. The Great Plains and the mountains were so well suited to the spread of wild horses that apparently some northern tribes acquired horses before the European humans arrived.

The story of Chief Joseph's horses which became the Appaloosa breed is well known. It might be appropriate to note that what the Appaloosa type was to the Nez Perce and the Shoshone, the Nokota horse was to the Sioux.

Lewis and Clark described the northern type Indian horses as "of an excellent race, lofty, elegantly formed, active and durable. Many of them look like fine English coursers and would make a figure in any country." These were experienced horsemen, describing quality.

Apparently the "northern mustang" developed as a bit larger than the wild horses of the southwest. Partly this may be due to the skillful selective breeding of the northern tribes.

A word about names, here. The "Sioux," (a French word) were a nation composed of three branches, Lakota, the largest, Dakota, from which the states are named, and Nakota, the smallest.

After the battle which bears the unfortunate Custer's name, Sitting Bull and many of the Lakota chiefs retreated into Canada, taking several hundred of their prized horses. Four years later, Sitting Bull returned to surrender to the U.S. Army in 1881, at Fort Buford, in North Dakota. His horses were confiscated and sold.

A French nobleman, the Marquis DeMores, bought 250 animals, aware of the desirability of the Sioux stock. As a matter of fact, ranchers throughout the entire area valued the Sioux mares (and still do) for breeding stock to produce cow horses.

Theodore Roosevelt wrote in glowing terms about this strain of horses, and used them on his North Dakota ranch, both as saddle horses and in "work" teams.

There were attempts to breed a bigger work horse by crossbreed-ing Indian mares to Percheron stallions, and to Thoroughbreds for saddle use. Many of these mares, it is said, carried scars from the battle with Custer's cavalry. These horses ran at large on open range, and there have been small "wild" herds in the area, since the early 1900s.

When the Theodore Roosevelt National Park was fenced in the 1950s, one herd was by chance confined in the Park. There have been varying policies since, including everything from preserving the strain to eliminating the horses from the Park entirely. It was not until the use of helicopters that it became possible to catch many of the hardy "northern mustangs." Present policy is to remove any horses from the Park in excess of forty animals.

In 1981, some thirty of these animals were obtained by the Kuntz ranch near Linton, North Dakota, in an effort to preserve the strain. In 1991, the breed was recognized with national registry status. There are over 200 registered animals now, with the major nucleus of breeding stock on the Kuntz ranch. It is possible to identify the original Andalusion type by blood testing. Experts describe these "Old-Line" horses as being "extremely divergent (in blood type) from all major groups of domestic breeds."

Frank and Leo Kuntz brought six animals to Des Moines for the Horse Fair, and I was impressed, more than I expected to be. The horses are good quality animals that should make excellent stock horses. They have powerful hind quarters, strong straight backs, and "elegant" heads, as Lewis and Clark said nearly two centuries ago. They are mostly blue roans, but a few red roans, blacks, and some have pinto markings. Many have white on the face. At the present time I would certainly not want to get back into the horse business. But if we were raising horses now, they would be Nokotas.

See you down the road.

What's in a Name?

Some time ago I noticed a TV news item, sort of a filler on a day when there wasn't much news. It was a short segment about a zoo, and I began to pay a little more attention. I'm fascinated by zoos, because I like animals. Zoos, big and little, are doing a great job of education and of helping preserve and restore endangered species.

This particular news segment wasn't that serious, but just a nice folksy thing with a bit of film about zebras. The thing that really caught my attention, and gave a chuckle that the segment wasn't really trying for was the name of one of the zebras: Spot. What a beautiful one line…Well, a one-*word* joke that needs no explanation at all. It's just there.

I once visited a zoo where they had a small herd of peccaries, the wild pigs of the southwest and Mexico. The sign on the fence told the name of one large male, Gregory Peccary. Another name for the same species is the Spanish javelina, and this was utilized in the name of Gregory's mate. Olivia DeHaviland was a popular actress at the time, so the female peccary was Olivia DeJavelina.

But pet names…I'm on thin ice here, because sometimes the names that our pets have had weren't too original. Usually I could blame the kids when they were small, but now I have to admit to a certain lack of imagination myself. Our Dalmatian is Spot. (Spot I was Spot, too, like Spot II. Sorry, I couldn't resist.)

We had just two barn cats a while back, a black one and a white one. They were called The Black One and The White One. Likewise, an old black brood cow, Blackie. To counteract that inane bit of imagery, I'll take credit for the name of our big brown cow: How-Now.

I think it was Edna who found a name for one of our present barn cats. This animal has a couple of odd dark marks over the eyes, which gives a constant expression of deep concern. Her name: Worry.

I mentioned the kids. We really had some strange names when they were small. A banty hen, for instance, named George. Our banty chickens ran loose, and George was a very good mother. She hid out her nest and raised innumerable broods of chicks for years. (That was interesting, because George was hatched in the house, just to see if we could incubate eggs. She knew all about mothering, though she'd never seen a mother hen. Her own mother was a light bulb!)

There was a series of turtles as the kids grew up. Usually they were named Turtie. It does seem that along the line one would have been named after the Dr. Seuss character, Yertil the Turtle, but as far as I can recall, none ever was.

I once knew a family who had a dog named Fido. The reason, they explained, simply that everyone knows Fido is a dog's name, but no one ever actually names a dog Fido. I once heard of a poodle by that name. However, this being a French poodle, they spelled it Phydeaux.

Bowser is another dog name. But, did you ever know a dog named Bowser?

Sometimes circumstances dictate the name of an animal, though. We once had a foal born on a cold January night. This was to be a special animal, sired by a national performance champion. The mare's previous foal had become a national champion at halter. We could hardly wait to see this foal. It was like waiting to open Christmas presents. It was a good foal, one of our best. But she was born on Friday the 13th. Her name? Lucky, of course.

(PS- I've had several inquiries about Miss Kitty, a kitten I wrote about last month. One of our daughters took her home, where she will be an indoor cat after all!)

See you down the road.

Nostalgia Ain't What It Was

The Wampus Cat

In last week's column I told about receiving a letter from a man who had been a youngster in one of my YMCA programs about (censored) years ago. In the course of the letter, he mentioned that among other leadership functions, I had "protected him from the wompus cat." That's the way he spelled it. I always thought it was "wampus," as in "catty-wampus," which everybody knew as a misalignment of something, preventing proper function. It's too bad that we've lost a lot of this sort of colorful language, but that's another story.

Back to the Wampus Cat...I spent several years in the field of outdoor recreation and youth camping, in a variety of settings. One thing that about all youth camping has in common is the campfire story. A campfire takes us back almost instantly to a setting much like that of ten thousand years ago. The light from the fire pushes back the shadows and all of the frightful creatures that lurk in the dark. For primitive Man these dangers were real, predators that were very seriously looking for a meal. This dread of the dark has been handed down to the present in our genetic inheritance. The psychologists refer to it as "racial memory." (As in "human race," not the illogical classification by skin color.) We can still imagine horrors out there in the dark that are more dreadful than any real ones.

Times are changing now. Few children are ever exposed to completely dark situations. They have to create monsters in the bathtub drain, which might nibble unsuspecting toes. But, I digress.

Nearly every camp I was ever associated with had its own scare story, to be told and retold season after season. Some were ghost stories, some dealt with wild animals. Sometimes, if there was a body of water nearby, some slimy unknown creature that rose up at certain times: A full moon, or dark and moonless...The story could be altered to match *tonight*. Let the listeners figure it out. Usually, a touch of the supernatural. A bear that can't be killed, or the disembodied spirit of a horse thief who was hanged "on that very tree over there." Possibly even, a short piece of frayed rope, placed there by the camp staff. Let the campers notice it.

Now all of this had a useful purpose, in addition to the deliciously self-inflicted scare. Even with a counselor supervising every eight or nine kids, there are usually some who want to evade authority. To sneak out of the cabin after the leader is asleep is a logical thing to try. But with a supernatural bear or the slimy thing from the lake out there in the dark, the lights out schedule found most campers safe inside the cabins. Very few campers dared to try to question the threat of the slimy creature or the ghost of the horse thief.

When I started my job in the "Boys' Department" of the Topeka Y, I found that the Y had a small and somewhat primitive camp a few miles south of town. Usually considered a "day camp," it was occasionally used for overnight or weekend programs. A World War II barracks building had been moved to the site and equipped with about 20 bunks, and a cook stove. It was also equipped with a baseball diamond and a traditional scare story, in this case, the Wampus Cat. It had been seen in the area since 1861, it was said. Descriptions varied with each sighting (and with each counselor who told the story.) Nearby neighbors still suffered the loss of a calf occasionally, etc. (it was said).

At another camp where I had worked earlier, a couple of us had devised a noise maker which we christened a "panther call," involving an empty gallon can and a leather boot lace. It seemed appropriate for this situation. By previous agreement with the counselors, I arrived after dark at about the time they wanted the campers inside for the night. I parked down the road, walked in to about fifty yards from the campfire, where stories were in progress, and gave a couple of yanks on the string of the panther call. Fortunately, no one was trampled in the rush back to the lodge.

I sauntered on in, and before entering, peeked in a window to see how things were going. By pure coincidence, a young camper looked out at the same moment. I couldn't avoid being seen, so I made a face and hissed at him, before going around to the door. A strange thing...We could never convince him that the face at the window was actually mine. He had *seen* the Wampus Cat.

See you down the road.

Random Stories July 1995

When I'm traveling around the West (or in any part of the country, for that matter), I treasure the stories I encounter. Many times my purpose for being there is as a speaker. Some of the stories and illustrations that I use will stimulate listeners to come over after the program to tell me their story.

Sometimes they're apologetic, but needn't be. I may use that story somewhere else. Even if I don't I'll remember and enjoy it. And in our part of the country, nearly every family has anecdotes and tales of early days. At least, if they've been here a generation or two.

An old man once told me about an adventure he had as a boy. He was out hunting rabbits in the snow with his .22 rifle, and encountered an armed man in the woods. The stranger wore a holstered pistol on his hip, not too unusual at the time. They talked, and the boy shot a rabbit or two. Then he missed one, and the stranger quickly drew his gun and dropped the running rabbit with one shot, picked it up and handed it to the youngster.

When he returned home with his booty, he related the experience to his parents, describing the stranger in detail.

"Son," his father told him, "that was Jesse James."

Was it? I don't know. That area of eastern Kansas and western Missouri is where the "James Gang" spent quite a bit of time. A lot of families have Jesse James stories, most of them true. So, even allowing for exaggeration, that one probably is.

Sometimes circumstances bring about a story. When I was a teenager I was riding on a bus in eastern Kansas when a thunderstorm swept in. Wind, rain, thunder and lightning, a typical summer storm but a bit more severe than average. Then hail began to fall. Small bounding pellets at first, but then larger chunks of ice. The driver stopped the bus. Baseball-sized hailstones were banging like bricks on the metal roof above us, bouncing around in a pretty frightening way. The elderly woman in the seat beside me became quite upset, jumping around each time one of the big hailstones struck.

Then it was over. The bus driver stepped out to pick up a few specimens. The passengers passed them around, marveling at their size until they melted.

My seat mate, now calmer, explained her reaction. She told in great detail how, as a child of eight or nine, she stood on the front porch of their farm home and watched as a man just fifty yards away was caught in the open and killed by hailstones.

Years later, I read somewhere that there is only one case on record of a human fatality from hail. If so, I had talked to an eyewitness! The story *was* pretty much the same.

One of my favorite stories, though, I picked up a few miles west of us, in the area where it happened. After a lecture, an older man approached and offered this story with an amused smile and a twinkle in his eye.

When he was a boy, he said, his dad was a cowboy who worked at a lot of different ranches. Finally he got a pretty good job which included a small frame house to live in. It actually had plastered walls, the best place they'd ever lived.

There was one major problem. Graffiti covered the white plaster. Scribbled fragments of poetry, sketches in pencil, charcoal, paint and who knows what. The boy's mother was scandalized. She could hardly wait to get to town to get some whitewash to repair the damage. Of course, he was very firmly admonished never to draw pictures on a wall. Then all the graffiti was obliterated by a pristine coat of white.

"I was sort of disappointed," the old man went on. "I was enjoyin' the pictures. There were horses and cowboys and cattle, Indians and buffalo...I really missed them."

I agreed that this was a remarkable story, and asked if they ever discovered who was responsible.

"Oh yes," he replied. "The folks asked around. It was some drunk cowboy named Fred Remington."

The artist's ranch, near Peabody, Kansas! I've talked to the people who live in that house now...The modern West isn't too far from the Old West, is it?

See you down the road.

Goldie

March 2001

I recently received a letter from a reader in another part of the state, which began in an unusual way: "Hi, Goldie!" There has been a lot of water down the river since I had been addressed that way. The writer went on to explain that his mother had called attention to an article about my writing. She also told him that I was the same person as the YMCA director who took him to camp with a group of other Topeka kids, about (censored) years ago. He's now a successful professional man.

After a great many years, his mother had completely blown my cover. But now, I guess it's time that the story can be told. It dates back to about the seventh grade, or even earlier. My parents had four children, all red-heads. My mother had light red hair, almost a strawberry blonde. Each of us had a slightly different tone of red, and mine was fairly light, about like my mother's. I took a bit of teasing about being a "carrot-top," but that was to be expected.

A substitute teacher started the trouble. A regular teacher was on sick leave, and in the course of learning our names, the new teacher called the roll each morning. About the third day, when I answered, she made an offhand remark: "Yes, I remember you, from your beautiful golden curls!" It was a cruel thing to do to a seventh grade boy. My alleged friends quickly dubbed me "Goldilocks," later shortened to merely "Goldie."

It wouldn't die. I hoped to lose it when our family moved to another town, but it was not to be. A year or two later at Camp Wood, the state YMCA camp, my new friends met some of my former (alleged) friends from the previous school. I attended Camp Wood as a camper for a few seasons, and eventually worked there as a counselor. By that time, there had been a lot of kids from all parts of the state who knew me as "Goldie." It was quite inconvenient, since it's pretty common to have people misunderstand the Coldsmith name anyway. During a hitch in the Army, I had no trouble with the nickname, though I was called "Red" sometimes. And, back home and in college, I was exempt from such indignity. However, I worked during the summers at Camp Wood, where there were people who still remembered. After graduation, I took a job as a director in the Boys' Division of the Topeka YMCA. A fresh start, where I'd be unknown, and would finally be rid of that nickname. Wrong! There had been Topeka kids at Camp Wood…When I arrived at the Downtown Y at an open house welcoming ceremony, there was a banner stretched across the entire boys' department.

WELCOME, GOLDIE!

I spent several years there, years with memorable events, mostly good, and then decided to go back to school to study medicine. (I've had several vocations.) Since I knew no one at all in the new setting, I kept my mouth shut about the nickname, and it *worked*. ("Free at last, free at last," to borrow a quote.)

I practiced medicine for 30 years, overlapping a few years with the writing profession, without being called "Goldie." I was pleased about that, because it would have seemed a bit undignified, I thought.

For a long time, magazine editors with whom I worked didn't even know I was a physician, much less my ill-fated history with nicknames. (That in itself is another story.)

My wife has never known me by "Goldie." Edna and I hadn't met until I was in medical school. I had told her about it, of course, but it was past history. Likewise, though my secretary has worked with me for about 18 years, she had never even heard the story. Both of them seemed to thoroughly enjoy the letter from the reader, whom I do remember as a kid in one of our YMCA boys' clubs. It's good to know that some of my young charges actually turned out well.

Possibly it's a mistake to have revealed a little-known fact about my past that would be best completely forgotten. But the story is too good *not* to use.

See you down the road.

A Ghost Story? April 2001

A few weeks ago I wrote about some of my experiences while working with young people in the YMCA. That stimulated some memories. Especially, those of campfire stories, some of which must traditionally be scary. Especially, during some autumn camp-outs, with Halloween just around the corner, ghost stories seemed appropriate.

We had YMCA clubs in several of the Topeka elementary schools, called "Grade Schools" then. Our clubs for boys were classified at grade school level as "Gra-Y" clubs as compared to Hi-Y and Junior Hi-Y clubs in High School and Junior High.

One of our active Gra-Y clubs was in a school whose enrollment was predominantly of "Spanish" extraction. This was a geographical coincidence, with really no segregation involved. A great many families of Mexican origin had people who worked for the A.T. & S.F. (Santa Fe Railroad, whose Eastern Division headquartered there.) One of my best counselors was assigned to that Gra-Y club. He was Anglo, but had a broad range of interest, and was beloved by the youngsters and their families. He picked up enough Spanish to do a lot of good work in that school situation. Though most of the kids had a fair command of English, they cherished an Anglo who would *try* to understand their ways.

Occasionally the Gra-Y clubs would plan an overnight excursion, and this leader loved such occasions, especially when that particular club was involved. They loved stories, and he was one of our best storytellers. I had driven out to see how they were getting along, and to listen to some of the stories around the campfire. Ghost stories… Everybody edged closer to the fire.

Part of the fun of a story fire is to involve anybody with a story to tell. So, when one of the eleven-year-olds offered to tell a ghost story, the alert counselor encouraged him to do so. This had actually happened to his father, the kid said. He had heard his dad tell the story to some other men. It had happened in Mexico, long before the kid's parents were married, the youngster related.

He was actually a pretty good storyteller for his age, and described in detail the ceremony of the "promenade." This custom is somewhat outmoded now, but was originally a semi-formalized method for teenagers and young adults to meet other singles of the opposite gender. It's a back-country custom, which I once saw carried out in a small town in the Philippines. The girls and young women, in best dresses, circle the plaza casually in one direction, while the young men, also attired for the occasion, circle the opposite way. They exchange smiles, greetings, and the woman indicates by a glance or a nod whether she's interested in meeting him. If so, the man may turn and walk with her or follow her to a place where they can get better acquainted.

In this case it was growing dark, and the young man was having no luck in trolling for a date. Then he noticed a pretty white dress he hadn't seen before. He didn't get a very good look, but was quite impressed, as he turned to follow the inviting nod of the head. The boy relating the tale was eloquent in his second-hand description of the beauty of this girl's hair and body and shapely legs, as told by his father. But, he related, she kept ahead of her suitor, down a dark street and into a small park away from traffic, still with enticing nods of the head. The tension mounted among the listeners...

"Then she turned...He saw her close up for the first time, and she had...The face of a *horse!*"

There was a gasp of horror from his young listeners.

I was never quite certain how many of those kids, if any, really understood that story. I do recall that the Gra-Y counselor and I were sore from laughing the next day. I'm sure that youngster could be a real storyteller by this time. His father surely was.

See you down the road.

The Chinese Puzzle

My grandpa used to refer to a knotty problem of any sort as being "like a Chinese puzzle." He had a few toys for visiting grandchildren to play with, kept in a small chest, "the toy box," under the bed. Many of these he had made, himself. He was especially fond of games, toys, and puzzles with moving parts. And, there was the Chinese puzzle. It was a sort of three-dimensional jigsaw puzzle, with several pieces. It was possible to move most of them, but until the key piece was in exactly the right position, none could be removed. Once you knew the trick, the puzzle could be reduced to a pile of sticks, and reassembled at will. It was all in knowing the secret of the Chinese puzzle.

I thought of that not long ago, when among the copious pile of daily junk mail, I noticed a sheet promoting a "Clinic for traditional Chinese medicine," in another city which I won't name. The phrase "all natural" caught my eye, which always raises suspicion, too. The attempt to imply that "natural" is synonymous with "better" or even "safe" is a bit frightening. A lot of things that are "natural" are lethal, too. I was also mildly suspicious that there were phrases such as "powerful alternative" and "magic herb," applied generously. The name of the specialist in traditional Chinese medicine (they didn't say "doctor") was not at all Chinese, but more suggestive of northern Europe. Well, I have no problem with that. The assimilation of other cultures is the way of the future.

Likewise with "herbal" remedies. Many of our present-day medicines are originally derived from plant sources. There are a couple of things that bother me about it, and which are closely related. One, there is no control or standardization of "herbal remedies." They are classed as food additives, so are under no food and drug regulation. Vitamins are in the same category. Misuse of "food additives" can be fatal.

Back to the clinic's flier...It was printed on both sides of the page, and my doubts increased when I noted no less than six misspelled words or major grammatical errors on just one side of the paper.

I began to study the phrasing in the wonderful effects claimed for these products. Usually it's possible to spot the gimmick which will allow a disclaimer in case of bad results. There was an impressive list of thirteen herbs with a description of their marvelous properties. I almost overlooked the fact that there was no claim or even a hint that any of these are included in the (all natural) "Magic Herb formula." It's simply a list of plants.

There were claims about "100% fat loss while still retaining muscle tissue." Another miracle substance "reduces LDL Cholesterol, promotes wound healing, acts as an antacid, helps control blood pressure, helps speed bone repair, etc., etc., etc.;" even "acts as an antibacterial." No documentation, of course.

Those are pretty big claims, and I was still looking for the key to the whole thing. There has to be a disclaimer somewhere. For a minute I thought I had it…"Rarely does an herb produce an unwanted side effect." Maybe the Chinese puzzle hinges on "rarely." Most plant-derived medicines are poisons in higher doses. Under "poisons" in the encyclopedia, there is a whole column of herbal poisons. Socrates was executed by being forced to drink hemlock. But I guess that wasn't an "unwanted" side effect.

I finally discovered the key, the blanket disclaimer which covers the extravagant claims and allows the tabloid-style (though illiterate) prose about these all natural wonder drugs. It was printed in very small, narrow white letters in a dark little square, beside large letters which shout "How to Order." The text, much more readable with a magnifying glass, states modestly: "These statements have not been evaluated by the Food and Drug Administration. These products are not intended to diagnose, treat, cure, or prevent any disease."

Thus ended the search for the key to the Chinese puzzle. It does raise other questions about those who may buy "these products." Wasn't it P.T. Barnum who observed that there's a sucker born every minute?

See you down the road.

Profanity, Vulgarity, and Obscenity   May 2001

A few weeks ago, a columnist in one of the weekly papers that we read had an article titled "The Gentleman Cow." I hadn't heard that expression for a while, but boy, do I remember it. My grandmother… But let's back up a bit…

During the 19th Century the entire English-speaking world was influenced by Britain's Queen Victoria. Great Britain had become a constitutional monarchy. The royal family was not held in high regard during the reigns preceding Victoria's elevation to the throne. The queen could only "warn, advise, or encourage" the prime minister, but Victoria was above reproach, having been carefully reared and educated in the dignity of the office. In modern parlance, she "hadn't been out much," but she was to become one of Britain's most greatly loved monarchs, and ruled for 63 years, until her death in 1901. By some strange quirk of human nature, her dignity and innocence seemed to bring out the best in her subjects. She wished them to become "high-minded, modest, self-righteous, and enterprising," and they responded, to the extent that the entire century is often labeled the "Victorian Era." Its influence lasted for half the next century.

To most people of my generation, the term invokes thoughts of a ridiculously extreme expectation of moral and ethical behavior. Anything bad, dirty, unprincipled, even sly or sneaky, was obviously unethical, and must be banished, punished, deplored, or denied. Vulgar words, and all reference to body functions or parts, especially those pertaining to reproduction, were absolutely taboo. There was a vast proliferation of cuss-word substitutes. Gosh, golly, G-whiz, gol-darn and so on replaced the name of the deity in profanity. Likewise, darn, dang, durn…In many popular novels, characters said things like "I'll be d——d." "Sonofagun" was pretty risque. As preacher's kids, my brother and I were completely forbidden to use any of the above substitutes, even.

Now, in an economy that was still pretty much agricultural, it seems remarkable that this persnickety denial extended even to animals' bodily functions and body parts. I was once told that "sweat" was a vulgar word. In a marginal usage, it could be said that animals sweat. People, however, "perspire," insisted that old lady.

As for the "gentleman cow," yes, my grandmother, born about 1855, used that term. "Bull" was absolutely unacceptable. We were also not allowed to say "pants" in her house. That was suggestive of undergarments, whose very existence was denied. We must say "trousers" or "knickers," as the case might be. (Shorts were, of course, unacceptable. She once ran her brother from California out of her house for entering, "half naked," in Bermuda shorts.)

She could fry chicken that would put the Colonel to shame, but her fried chicken carried strange nomenclature, because of the body parts hangup. As I recall, neck, wing, back, and drumstick were permissible, but these chickens had no breasts, legs, thighs, or tails. It was okay to say white meat. I have heard ladies of that vintage refer to a chicken "limb." Even a piano couldn't have "legs." The fried chicken "tail" was a favorite of my brother's, but he had to refer to it as "the part that goes over the fence last."

Reference to the male of domestic animals, which started this train of thought, is oddly uneven. It was okay to say "rooster" or "tom-cat," but not "bull" or "buck" or "boar" or "stallion." And among canines, it's the female who gets the bad press, as in the literary term "son of a b——," watered down to "sonofagun." I'll never understand that one, but still have trouble *saying* it, even now, and even in legitimate usage.

By contrast, my army basic training was with mules, and mule skinners were traditionally felt to be the world's most expert cussers. We had a sergeant who was said to have been able to swear for three minutes straight without repeating himself. I've heard him come pretty close. Sarge was a world-class cusser. I think he held a Black Belt in the event.

But the pendulum swings. Having heard about every cuss word there is as a mule packer, I still cringe now at some of the language in movies or on prime time TV. I'm sure that Queen Victoria is rotating in her grave.

See you down the road.

The Dowsers

Just before the holidays, a friend handed me an article he'd taken off the internet. We don't use the internet, for about three good reasons: *One*, I'd waste time. (I do that, even with encyclopedias and dictionaries. Something else will look interesting, and I stop to read that, which leads to something else, and...) *Two*, it's not reliable for research. Anybody can put anything on the internet, valid or pure lies. Any fact must be verified by more research, so to do both would waste time again. I'd rather do the research first, and forget the internet. *Three*, I'm sort of a dinosaur, resistant to a lot of changes which fail to impress me as improvements. "If it ain't broke, don't fix it."

Yes, I do use the computer for a thousand pages or so of book manuscript each year, but my long-time secretary operates it. My part is by hand, with a beat-up mechanical pencil which has produced at least a half-dozen novels. (And...we'll soon have as a promotional tool, a new web page: DonColdsmith.com)

But, back to the internet print-out handed to me at church. Its title is intriguing: "Grave Dowsing." The article is four pages long, with detailed instructions for making dowsing rods out of a couple of coat hangers. The purpose, stated in the article, is to assist in locating unmarked graves when doing genealogical research. (I'm not sure how that would help, but maybe...) There were hints about how to determine age, sex, and orientation of a buried body by the behavior of the dowsing rods.

"What do you think of this sort of thing?" asked my friend.

Well, I'm not sure what I think, except that there is something to it. Dowsing is an old term, and is probably more preferable to the alternate, also ancient, "witching." It really has nothing to do with witchcraft or satanic cults or ceremonies. Witching was considered, on the frontier, a perfectly reasonable way to locate where to dig the well for a new homestead. Some people were better at it than others, and most communities had a "water witch." It wasn't steady employment, of course. Just a special skill, as another might be better at stacking hay or plowing a straight furrow. (The grave-dowsing article, incidentally, states that more than 90% of the population can utilize this dowsing technique, some better than others.)

As a small boy, I watched my grandfather use this method, (for water, not for bodies.) He explained to me in detail. Wire coat hangers weren't mentioned, but various varieties of green wooden sticks. Many people, he said, swear by witch-hazel. This, of course, gives the shrub its name. But in areas where witch-hazel doesn't grow, you have to use something else. His favorite was a forked branch from a young peach tree. Others, he said, prefer willow, especially for water, willows having an affinity for water anyway. But whatever, it must be green and flexible. He had stories of such a mighty pull on the stick by the "draw" of an underground stream that the slippery green bark of the branch was broken loose. I didn't see that, but have heard the same story several times from others.

This whole idea of witching (or "dowsing," for those uneasy about evil forces) has a unique appeal. We also have to take a look at the concept of a "good" witch, a la the Wizard of Oz, or favorable spiritual influences such as "gifts of the spirit." I see nothing threatening here. Dowsing is alive and well. Only a few years ago I met a dowser who worked in the oil fields, a full time professional. He was highly respected by the drillers. His equipment was a far cry from a coat hanger or a peach stick, though. His dowsing rod consisted of a pair of chrome-plated springs like the old screen-door spring, attached in a Y to a small chamber with a screw top. Each spring had a rubber grip at the end, to be grasped exactly the way my grandfather held the peach fork. This dowser also wore a sort of a cartridge belt, with compartments which held small bits of whatever substance he might need to dowse for: Water, oil, coal, gold, silver, lead, zinc…You name it, each sample in a tiny vial that could be fitted into the screw-top chamber of the instrument, depending on what he needed to dowse today. He tried to demonstrate for me, but it didn't work. Some of his no-good friends had switched vials on him. At least, that's what he said.

See you down the road.

End of the Garden

November 1996

By the time you read this, we'll have had the first frost of the season. Gardeners will be cleaning up the last of the fresh home-grown tomatoes, storing winter squash, and making pickles with the last of the cucumbers. A few will have picked the green tomatoes at the last minute, maybe fried a few, or set them aside to ripen in a paper bag. They'll do that. They're not as good as vine-ripened, of course, but much better than the styrofoam tomatoes we get from the store through the winter.

I had an aunt who was a great gardener. She had to be. They farmed forty acres for a living, with horse teams, and did pretty well at it. One of her recipes was for "End-of-the-garden Pickles." As I remember it, she sort of chopped up about everything that she could salvage and pickled it with vinegar, salt, and spices. Green tomatoes, sweet peppers, a few onions, summer squash, cucumbers…It was pretty good. It seems to me that she sometimes put a few carrots in it, too, to give it a little color. Or maybe that was just from red bell peppers. I never thought about it very much as a kid.

One major advantage to this time of year is that we don't have any zucchini squash to worry about until next summer. I don't really hold any grudge against zucchini, you understand. It's just that there's always a surplus. Sure, it's nice to have an easily-grown vegetable that produces in abundance. However, if we're going to produce a surplus, it would be nice if it were something with a certain amount of flavor.

But a zucchini *does* have flavor, I heard someone say. Sure, so does a lettuce sandwich on white bread, but not much. (At a fraternity house where I ate lunch while in school, the cook occasionally served lettuce sandwiches. They were referred to as Ella's "nothin' sandwiches" by the young men who boarded there.)

In zucchini season, there are always a great many recipes in newspapers and magazines, with suggestions about what to do with zucchinis. One paper whose pages I always glean for good recipes had an issue with nothing but zucchini recipes. (Is this a sign of desperation?)

There were eight or ten of them, ranging from stir-fry to soups to a chocolate zucchini cake.

I have no doubt that some of these were pretty good. A daughter of ours came home not long ago and brought a delicious apple pie. One of the best I ever ate, in fact. It wasn't until we finished that, over coffee, she explained that it wasn't an apple pie, but zucchini! Its true nature had been cleverly disguised by parboiling and the addition of a lot of lemon juice, cinnamon, nutmeg, and sugar. It was tremendously successful, and I certainly hope that any opinion expressed here will not prevent her from bringing pies when she comes again. Even zucchini pie.

But think about it: Look at all the recipes with ways to dispose of zucchinis. Is there any significance in the fact that nearly every zucchini recipe in the world has as its ultimate purpose to get rid of zucchini, and make it resemble something else? What does that tell us, about zucchini or about ourselves? I thought of the old truism that "if there are more than four ways to do a thing, it's certain that none of 'em are worth a damn."

A while back I was lecturing in a small western Kansas town. I like an audience of that kind, and towns of that kind. They don't have the problems that we see in the cities. They don't bother to lock their houses when they go to the store, many times. I remarked on this to the man who was to introduce me after we finished the covered-dish dinner we were eating. I asked if they even locked their cars when they were in town.

"Well, no," he assured me. "Except, of course, in zucchini season."

See you down the road.

Musical Reunion   September 1996

Fifty years ago, I was just back from the Army, and enrolled in college at Baker University. On a bulletin board I saw a notice of try-outs for a male quartet. I had sung in church choir and high school chorus, so I decided to wander over and watch the tryouts. Before I knew it, I had not only tried out, but had made the team. I had to drop a couple of other things, but this looked like fun. The other three members were complete strangers, both to me and to each other. However, this set up a couple of the most interesting years of our lives.

The Baker University Men's Quartet (spelled "quartette" then), was a tradition at Baker, I learned. They sometimes performed at schools and churches in the area, and informally promoted the University to aid recruitment.

Our harmony seemed to happen instantly and comfortably. Our director was the chairman of the Music department, William Rice, who seemed excited about our blend and encouraged us to try some of our own ideas. We did.

At that time, a lot of the top recording groups were male quartets, or other small vocal combos. These ranged from western to blues to religious to pop, and even light classical. There's a tendency now to think: "Male quartet...Barbershop." But that wasn't the case. We did a little of everything, including barbershop, spirituals, religious songs, and even a pretty racy number or two from current Broadway shows. In addition, I knew a lot of camp songs as a result of having worked as a YMCA camp counselor for several years. We used some of those, creating our own arrangements.

Oddly, only one of us was a music major, our top tenor, Bill Cofer. Our bass, Frank Leitmaker, was pre-med, Bill Soper, lead tenor, was a business major, and I was in psychology. (As a student, not in therapy). We were assigned a piano accompanist for accompanied numbers...The first year, Ruth Reichley, the second Carol Vandegraft. Both were excellent pianists, and as one might expect, put up with a lot of flak from the quartet.

We traveled a lot, eventually nearly every weekend, and once or twice a year on a week-long tour, performing several times a day. We put on several radio shows at WDAF in Kansas City. Near the end of our second year, we were offered a chance to go on the road as professionals, for a summer tour. We were still considering when the agent involved signed a another quartet for the contract, a "big name" group. Soon after that, two of our members graduated, one married, and it was all over but memories. I nearly abandoned music, due to time pressures. We all but lost track of each other.

Until now, almost exactly fifty years later…Frank, now a retired Army physician, married and living in Germany, was to be in the area for a Barbershop function. He's in the Barbershop movement in Germany. (Yes, it's worldwide.) With Frank's prodding, we located everybody involved, and on an August weekend, held a reunion at Bill Soper's home in Columbia, Missouri. Everyone was there, except our director, Dr. Rice, and Ruth, one of the accompanists, now living in Idaho. Ruth sent her greetings on an audiotape, and we phoned Dr. Rice, whose health wouldn't permit a visit. Carol brought us all photocopies of her scrapbook with newspaper clips from all over, about our performances. Frank brought T-shirts with a picture of the group "the way we were." Mrs. Soper was a wonderful hostess, and fed us a marvelous lunch.

We listened to ourselves on tape…I have a couple of old $33\frac{1}{3}$ records of "air-checks" from our radio shows, and Bill Cofer had taped a copy for each of us. We still agreed…Yes, we must have been pretty good.

This theory was borne out by the reactions of a friend of Frank's. He's a capable young barbershopper who came along to meet us and see if we wanted to sing a little. (We did, but not much.) At one point, he said as he listened, "You guys did this arrangement?" Another time, simply "Wow!" I figured that was a pretty good compliment.

All in all, a special reunion.

See you down the road.

The Plum Thicket September 1994

When we first moved to our present home, more than thirty years ago, it was well outside of town. We bought the twenty-five acres for pasture, and the old farmstead for a homesite. There were seven in our family, and we needed a little more room, indoors and out. We built the house two years later. Our water supply was an old well with a pump in a pit nearby. We have a rural water line now.

There was no other human habitation in sight. Our nearest neighbor was a quarter mile to the west, but we couldn't see his house. There was a shallow ravine, a small timbered area, and a dense thicket of wild plums, just across the fence on our neighbor's place. It was the plum thicket that really formed the west wall of our little world. For most of the rest we had horizon, broken by a few trees here and there.

In the pasture behind the house we often saw wildlife. Once, a couple of the kids and I went for a little hike in a new snow, to look for tracks. We followed a rabbit's trail, and saw it joined by a coyote's track. There were signs of pursuit and scuffle, and blood on the snow. It seemed pretty fresh, and we followed the coyote tracks a little way, to find a fresh-killed rabbit, still warm, stuffed in a hollow tree. We figured that we must have been so close that the hunter hid his kill and departed, to come back later for dinner.

Through the years we've also seen deer, wild turkeys, raccoons, possums, a fox family who raised a litter of pups behind the house, innumerable quail, a nesting pair of pheasants, and heard a bobcat's scream in the night.

And there was the plum thicket. There is only one springtime smell nicer than the scent of plum blossoms in early spring. (Wild grape blossoms have a slight advantage, and we have those, too.) Plums are among the first of the wild blooms, just before the redbud trees, and often together. This one was a growth of pure plums, though. We could sit on the back porch and see and smell and enjoy.

A little later in the season the edge of that thicket was a good place to look for mushrooms. Morels, one of the tastiest, best and safest of the wild mushrooms.

The plum thicket contributed greatly to our environment, too. It was a shelter for many of the creatures I've mentioned. There was always a covey of quail there every season. Deer came from the timber along the river, crossed our pasture, and often disappeared into the deep shade of the plum thicket to spend the daylight hours. In later years, turkeys have responded to good management, and we've seen them cross our yard to that brushy thicket and back.

In late summer, of course, there were the plums. Good for wildlife and for people, for eating or for jelly. That use is a whole 'nother story.

Then in autumn, my favorite time of the year, there are a few glorious days when the wild plums and the wahoo bushes show their wonderful color . Yellows, orange, pinks, and reds. We'd sit on the porch and note the change from one evening to the next.

Even in winter the thicket was attractive, with drifted snow and the thick stems furnishing shelter to quail and rabbits and the occasional deer.

Over the years, our horizon has occasionally been violated by new construction. I've planted strategically located trees to minimize the overall effect, with some success. Eventually, of course, the place to the west of us changed hands. The old man who was our neighbor has been gone for years. Finally, the inevitable. A house, a big one, just a stone's throw from the coyote's kill in the snow…There are no coyotes now. I planted more trees.

We returned from a trip out of town this summer to hear the sounds of a chain saw and a bulldozer to the west of us. The new owner was "landscaping" the property. All remaining trees were trimmed and pruned to several feet above the ground. The "brush" was cleared, and the plum thicket was gone.

From the porch, when we look westward, we see the ravine, between tree trunks. There's no cover or shelter for quail or turkeys or deer. I hope the new owner enjoys his view. I guess that's progress.

Meanwhile, I'm planning to plant a plum thicket on our side of the line. A few years…

See you down the road.

Smells of Childhood June 1994

We were sitting on the screen porch one evening in early May, enjoying the sunset. It was especially pleasant, because the weather had been strange. Hot, cold, rainy, sometimes all in the same day. We had just had a really late nip of frost. (I don't remember any other year in my lifetime when our asparagus froze back to the ground *after* we'd harvested the first batch.)

So, this was nice, almost the first evening we'd been able to sit on the porch. It was warm. There was the smell of freshly-mown grass in the yard. That's always a good smell, though it gets a bit less attractive when we're mowing in September. But for now, it signals the beginning of warm weather.

There were other scents, a variety of them. We'd had a nice gentle shower earlier, and had remarked on that smell. The white spirea blossoms were opening, and honeysuckle behind the house.

Then the breeze shifted a little and we caught the sweet scent of lilies-of-the-valley from across the patio. We both said something about it at exactly the same time. After a certain number of years together, a couple begins to do that.

Edna has always loved that scent. She associates it with her birthday, May first. That was the day she was permitted to begin going barefoot each year, as a child. A handy mile post!

I had always thought that there must have been a bed of lilies-of-the-valley at her childhood home in Weleetka, Oklahoma. But she said no, it was a bottle of perfume that someone gave her, with that fragrance. Yet each year, when the lilies-of-the-valley bloom, their unmistakable scent transports her back to childhood, her birthday, Oklahoma, a gift of perfume for a little girl. Similarly, the scent of peonies belongs with Memorial Day.

I've written about this before, but it will stand another look. There's some scientific evidence that of our various senses, smell has the strongest tendency to jog our memory. Back, all the way to earliest recall and maybe before. Sometimes we'll encounter a scent that we know well, but just can't quite remember…But it gives a feeling of pleasure or concern or fear. Usually it's a pleasant recall, because memory has a protective feature. We have a tendency to forget the unpleasant and save the pleasurable experience to recall and think about and treasure. So, it's recalled more easily by an associated scent.

Sure, there are some undesirable memories. The odor of menthol always recalls for me a certain custom from my childhood, until about the time I started to school. If I had a cough, my mother rubbed my skinny little chest with a magic healing ointment, Mentholatum. It was smelly and sticky and I didn't like it, but that memory is easily stirred.

Better ones include bread baking or bacon frying. Wood smoke from the cook stove on the farm of an aunt and uncle. Apples or quinces in the fall, and the smell of roasting turkey with sage stuffing at Thanksgiving. Cinnamon or cloves bring sensations of warmth and protection. Frying onions are powerful, too.

It's not always food, though. Wild plum thickets beckon to adventure. So does the clean, wild smell of a free flowing river. New-mown hay.

The smell of a clean, dry stable on a hot day takes me back to the Army mule barns at Fort Sill, Oklahoma. I started basic training there one summer quite a few years ago. It's not a totally unpleasant animal smell, and always recalls that period of my life, which brought a lot of excitement and adventure as well as hard work.

Another Army memory is triggered by the smell of jasmine. That was in Fort Benning, Georgia. I was on night guard duty, in an old, beautifully landscaped part of the post. It was a warm, moonlit night, still and beautiful. It was like being transported back a century in time to the Old South. Nobody bothered me for the entire guard shift, and the memory is good, recalled by the scent of the jasmine hedge along an old flagstone walk.

I went overseas shortly after that, and was subjected to an assortment of smells not nearly so nice. Fortunately, not scents that are frequently encountered.

Lilies-of-the-valley for me? Oh, those were on the north side of my grandmother's house in Iola, Kansas. I remember one time…

See you down the road.

High School Reunion November 1993

We recently attended a high school reunion. Mine. We had attended Edna's before, and I always enjoyed them. She went to school with some pretty interesting people. But I had never been back to Coffeyville for a high school reunion.

Maybe the old saying about "you can't go back" was part of it. Maybe it was the fact that when I returned from the Army I went directly to college. My parents had moved away, leaving no ties there. Or maybe it was that I was a little slow to develop in adolescence. I was a little fat kid during most of high school. I sure wasn't part of the in-crowd. I wasn't big enough to go out for football until my senior year.

That was when one of the varsity football players talked me into it. We had a good team. Conference champions and all that. There were twelve seniors from last year's squad, a few of whom were on the state all-star roster. Prominent among those were a couple of offensive linemen. I was a second (or third) string end, so I routinely played against the varsity in practice scrimmage. I'd come around the line and those all-state linemen would half kill me. Then the coach would run the play again and again, until they were doing it to me like he wanted it done. I never actually got into a game.

I was finally required to choose between football and band. That was easy. Playing a piccolo seemed less hazardous to my health.

This high school anniversary was a big one, with a zero on it. (Not 20, either.) This one, Edna insisted, we were going to attend, so I finally agreed.

It was a unique experience. Some of those who were pretty close friends weren't there. One had season tickets to the Chiefs games, he'd told the organizers. (Well, okay, if he'd rather see Joe Montana.) There was one of my best friends who apparently wasn't even in my class, which surprised me some. He must have been a year ahead of me.

Some of the jocks were fat and bald, some of the cheerleaders weren't nearly as attractive. Actually there were a lot of old people there. I really did feel that Edna and I looked better than any of them, though. But a couple of the men actually looked better than they did in school. More dignified.

People kept commenting that I had been younger than the rest of the class. I was sure that they had me confused with my brother, who was three years younger. I said so, a couple of times, until Edna suggested I tell them sure, I was, and let 'em eat their hearts out.

We had a good time, though. We had dinner with one of the offensive linemen who used to maul me every afternoon, and his nice wife. He didn't look as big as he used to.

One of my friends, called "Scrug" in school, is a retired school administrator. They don't call him Scrug now. His wife, a year or two younger, was a girl I dated once or twice. She had a charming nickname, bestowed by her parents when she was small. They don't call her Sugar-Beth any more, either, I guess.

In talking to others of my former classmates, we made some interesting observations. There were about 250 in our class of '43, but we only graduated 236. Several dropped out to enter the military. World War II was in full swing, and most of the men went directly into the Armed Forces. Some of the women went into college or into wartime jobs. The rest scattered. There was little opportunity to stay in contact for a few years, with the war moving everyone around, and the class of '43 simply lost touch with each other.

In recent years, they've sort of regrouped, I guess. This was the biggest reunion so far. There were about 170, I think, but that included spouses. If I had to estimate, possibly as many as a hundred actual graduates. Not a bad average.

It was a great weekend. Wonderful food, a big band that played "our" dance music from the '40s. Good music, not so loud it cracks your glasses and your eardrums.

See you down the road.

Groundhog Day

When I was a pretty small kid, quite a few years ago, we were visiting relatives one winter day. This was on an old family farm near Mound Valley, Kansas. My maternal grandparents were there for the day. Although Grandpa had once farmed this place, they now lived in town and an aunt and uncle were on the farm.

Grandpa always reverted to type when he was on the farm, though. He'd be in and out of the house, bringing in wood or corncobs for the kitchen stove, or carrying water from the well. There was no electricity or inside plumbing.

It had started to snow a little, and the ground was getting white. Grandpa came into the kitchen with an armload of wood, stamped the snow off his boots, and tossed a casual question to the three or four youngsters there by the stove.

"Ever see any red snow?"

This stopped me for only a moment. I knew my grandfather pretty well. He was a tease, but he had one inviolable rule: he never said anything that was not completely and undeniably true.

My younger brother, not quite as sophisticated as I in Grandpa's ways, swallowed the joke whole. Hook, line, and sinker. "Where?" he hollered, heading for the door. He was prevented from opening the door just in time by various female relatives. They were not anxious to have the wintry blast come through the kitchen again.

My brother, you see, had realized that Grandpa always told the truth. He didn't quite have the rest of it figured yet. He hadn't noticed that Grandpa didn't actually *say* there was red snow out there, but merely asked if we'd seen any.

There was another time, though, when he completely suckered me. We were at Grandpa's that time, and had stayed overnight. Breakfast was always wonderful there. My Grandma made big fluffy soda biscuits about two inches tall...but that's another story. This time we were eating biscuits and comb honey, with eggs and country sausage. It was February second. We were talking about Groundhog Day, wondering if the little critter would see his shadow, thus deferring the coming of spring by six more weeks.

I'm never quite sure how that works when February second is a partly cloudy day. What if a woodchuck on our place sees his shadow, but one a mile or two away doesn't? That must take some pretty intricate timing…

Anyway, we talked about it for some time, there at breakfast, how that's why February second is called Groundhog Day. "And that's why we're eatin' it," said Grandpa casually.

"Eatin' *what?*" demanded my brother suspiciously.

"Oh, Daddy!" scolded my mother.

My sister started to gag a little, turned green, and pushed back from the table. She always gagged pretty easy, though.

"Well, it is," Grandpa said defensively, his blue eyes twinkling as he took another bite of sausage. "Ground hog."

My sister was in the bathroom by that time, and it was apparent that we needn't save any more sausage for her.

A lot of years later, I pulled the same thing on our kids. We had five girls, of course, and I managed to evoke the same "Oh, Daddy!" scolding from a couple of them, while the younger ones peered at their plates suspiciously. Nobody gagged or ran for the bathroom, though. Our kids had pretty strong stomachs.

Actually, sausage made from woodchucks wouldn't be all that bad. I once tasted a roast woodchuck and it was pretty good. Sausage has undoubtedly been made of vastly worse ingredients many times.

See you down the road.

March is a Slob March 1993

Quite a few years ago, a lady I know made a statement about March. When her time comes, she said, she hoped it would be in February, so she wouldn't have to go through the month of March again.

March is pretty unpleasant in our part of the country. Unpredictable, changeable, different things to different folks, and in different parts of the United States. In some areas, it's somewhat pleasant, I understand. Some individual days might be in the plains, but they can't be trusted.

Baxter Black once suggested changing the name of this month to "Mud…" ("Doesn't sound much different, does it?" he asked in a column dated "Mud 7, 1985.")

In the deep south, Black reported, they actually enjoy March. But here, he went on, "The March rain…is not a gentle, life-giving shower from Heaven to be savored and sniffed. It's more like the angels hosing out their confinement hog shed."

Well, I can relate to that, and to the mud theory. This is one of the easiest months to get a tractor stuck. You can't do any planning, because there's no way to tell whether it will be sunny, windy, pouring rain, blowing snow, or breaking up trees and power lines with ice by the ton covering everything. You have to take it a day at a time because it will be different tomorrow anyway, and at best it will probably be whang-leather tough and freeze up solid on most nights. You can't do much but look forward to April.

When we were raising horses it was often the beginning of the competition season for a horse show or two. I'd wonder sometimes why we'd subject ourselves to something like that. I still don't know, except that people with animals *do* that kind of thing. Subject themselves to misery, that is. I recall one year when we pulled the big horse trailer out of the mud with a "come-along" hand winch, just to get it to where we could hitch it to the pickup. Then we were ready to haul hairy horses to a competition where we'd surely get beaten. I could never figure how our halter horses were the last in the Great Plains to shed winter hair and look sleek and ready. This was in spite of keeping them blanketed, inside, well fed, and doing a lot of "spring horse cleaning" with a curry comb. They'd still have the "hairy side out."

Now, we worry more about new calves, in rain and cold and snow and wind-chill indices at about zero. Sometimes you can't do much except hope for the best, which may be none too good.

"If March was a person," to quote one more Baxterism, "it would be an old man...The kind that won't turn up his hearing aid or zip his fly." (What a way with words! Wish I'd said that.)

Despite all this, there have been several cultures that saw March as the beginning of the new year. The Awakening, resurrection, new growth, new birth, and so on. Well, yes. March is somewhat like having a new baby in the house. As I recall, there *were* sleepless nights and diapers and all. There's an analogy here. Fortunately, babies grow out of some of that. Usually, anyway.

And, I guess, so does March. Things do get better.

Now about the lady I mentioned at the beginning. She hasn't mentioned the advantages of dying in February for a number of years. One February she did nearly die, and logged some time in the intensive care unit. That sort of put things in a different light. I have an idea that when she woke up, she was thinking something like "Hey, I was only kidding! Sorry, I won't say it again." Anyway, she hasn't.

See you down the road.

The Buffalo Soldier June 1993

In the past year or two, there has been an increased interest in an almost forgotten part of the history of the Great Plains, the "Buffalo Soldier." It's of special interest to Kansans, because the home base of these units was at Fort Riley, the Cavalry School of the United States Army.

The Buffalo Soldiers' story goes back to the Civil War. After the war ended, the United States was in a situation with several special features of a temporary nature. This was a time when the principle of "Manifest Destiny" was strong. In simplest terms, that theory promoted the idea that it was the will of God that the United States grow westward in uninterrupted possession to the Pacific Ocean. A major problem was the fact that there were already people living there.

It would obviously, then, require some military force and perhaps what we now call "ethnic cleansing," to carry out the will of God. The Army was at low ebb, through combat, and the return of the wartime troops to civilian life, both in the North and the South.

There was another problem, however, in the thousands of freed slaves with nowhere to go and nothing to do. Many of these were adult males, accustomed to hard work and obeying orders. These are qualities which also make good soldiers, and in fact, there had been some black units in the Union Army during the war. Why not, somebody reasoned, help to solve both problems at once? Form regiments of black soldiers with white commanders and black non-commissioned officers? The result was the formation of the 9th, 10th, 11th, and 12th Cavalry, to operate on the frontier helping to subdue the "Wild West."

To scheme was pretty successful. The Negro units *were* good soldiers, tough fighters, and they played a big part in the "expansion period." In fact, there were Negro units in all the wars that the United States fought, clear up through the Korean Conflict. But the nickname that was applied to the black cavalrymen in the 1860s had a tendency to stick: "Buffalo Soldiers."

The Indians of the Great Plains were astonished by the first black troops they saw. They had already seen a few black frontiersmen, and the Indian hand signs for a Negro indicate "black white man." But whole *troops* of soldiers, *all* blacks…

There's a tendency to rewrite history a little bit right now. I've read recently that the Indians coined the term "Buffalo Soldier" because these troops were "strong and courageous," like the buffalo. My Indian friends, however, tell it a little bit differently. It was because they *looked* like a buffalo, *and* were strong and courageous). The curly hair, dark skin…But remember, the Indians who fought against the Buffalo Soldiers were the hunters of the Great Plains. To them, the buffalo was not only the basis of their culture and their economy, but part of their religion, a sacred animal. The term Buffalo Soldier was the highest of honors. All this came to mind when I heard of the recent death of a disabled U.S. Army veteran in a nursing home in St. Mary's, Kansas. His name was Oscar Williams, and he was 98 years old.

Oscar had enlisted in the cavalry to fight World War *One*. He was a member of one of the black "Buffalo Soldier" troops. After a few months he was involved in an accident, permanently disabled when he was kicked in the head by a horse.

He became a ward of the government. While he did not require hospitalization, he could not function in society, and lived in a succession of care homes for the rest of his life. His affairs were managed by an appointed conservator. There are only distant relatives left now, but Oscar does have some friends. Interested people are trying to see that this veteran Buffalo Soldier is put to rest with appropriate honors in a military cemetery.

See you down the road.

The Old Trooper

I had a speaking engagement in Leavenworth last month. A friend who lives there had suggested that it would be a good time to visit the fort and see the new monument to the Buffalo Soldiers.

I've written about the Buffalo Soldiers before. These were Negro cavalrymen of the 9th and 10th Regiments, formed in 1866, under the command of white officers. These units underwent no major changes in organization until World War II, and became officially racially integrated in 1952.

The "Buffalo Soldier" name was bestowed by the Indians who faced black troops on the prairies of the Great Plains. Curly hair, dark skin... To people whose religion considered the buffalo sacred, this was a very important thing. At first it must have appeared that these white men had painted themselves ceremonially to look like the buffalo. But when it was discovered that they had been born that way, it placed the black "warrior" a notch above white men. In fact, the Indian hand sign for a Negro translates literally: "black white man." They were given special respect by their Indian opponents. The Buffalo Soldier name stuck, and remained in common use on the frontier, and into modern times.

The monument and the bronze statue of a black cavalryman of the 10th Regiment stands on the post at Fort Leavenworth. It overlooks the old barracks and the stables there in a fitting tribute to the contribution of these soldiers. We visited the site in a drizzling rain, but the day was brightened considerably by the gentleman who accompanied us there.

Our friend had managed to arrange for us to meet one of the surviving Buffalo Soldiers, Harry H. Hollowell, Chief Warrant Officer, Retired. Mr. Hollowell served in the 10th from 1936 to 1942, when reorganization took place. He then attended the Army Music School and became a bandmaster, serving both overseas and in the continental US until his retirement in 1964. However, I'm sure he thinks of himself as a trooper of the 10th Cavalry.

He was dressed in a cavalryman's uniform. Not the olive drab of the 1930s when he enlisted, but the blue and gray of the original

Buffalo Soldier of the plains. He wore the yellow kerchief around his neck, and still stands ramrod straight, looking about 20 years younger than I know he is.

We had stopped by the Hollowell's home first, met his charming wife Velma, and watched a couple of short videotapes about the Buffalo Soldiers, the ground-breaking ceremony, and the dedication of the statue later. General Colin Powell, Chairman of the Joint Chiefs of Staff, was present. The memorial had been a pet project of his.

We looked at some of Mr. Hollowell's memorabilia, and then we all drove out to the fort. It started to rain about the time we got out to walk around the memorial. We had raincoats and umbrellas, and it wasn't raining too hard, so we went ahead with it.

The old trooper had now added to his dress. An old blue felt hat of 1860s Army pattern, with yellow braid and crossed sabers insignia... A long Army raincoat. He was still in character.

The memorial itself is beautiful, the statue of the horseman inspiring. Every detail, down to the equipment, saddle and bridle. Even the horse's brands, a 10 for 10th Regiment on the left hip and a US on the left shoulder, appear authentic.

There's a pond behind the horseman, and a little waterfall into a pool below. The landscaping includes native prairie grasses, the whole thing really well done.

Mr. Hollowell pointed out the barracks where he'd lived as a trooper, the middle one of a trio of brick buildings about a rifle shot from the monument. Beyond that, the old stables...

We got back in the car for a swing around the post. The old Command and General Staff School, some newer buildings.

The old trooper led the way down an asphalt street with a sign which read 9th Cavalry Street, and back around through 10th Cavalry Street. A few years ago, these were only gravel paths, the only sign of the forgotten black troopers. But now they, along with the Buffalo Soldier himself, have attained some recognition, and assumed a rightful place in American history.

It was a good day.

See you down the road.

Travelin'

Out Where the West Begins October 1995

This past summer there was a story on the Associated Press line about whether Kansas should be considered West or Midwest. The headline on the article read "Where is Kansas?"

There were quotes from several "authorities," only one of whom is a Kansan. The others were academics from Utah and New Mexico, so would hardly qualify. Add to that the fact that no two descriptions of "Midwest" have ever been alike anyway.

The general theme of this article seemed to say that there are two parts of Kansas, divided along the 98th meridian or the 100th, depending on the authority being quoted. The 98th would put the Flint Hills and such cow towns as Abilene in the Midwest. The other theory would put everything east of Dodge City outside the West. (We might mention that Kansas originally extended west to the Continental Divide and included Denver. It was lopped off to add to Colorado even before they started stealing our water.)

But let's look at what is the West, anyway. To the first American frontiersmen, Daniel Boone, Davy Crockett, et al, the West was western New York, Pennsylvania, Kentucky, and Tennessee. In literature of the frontier, the stories start there.

Zane Grey, one of the greatest authors of the West, set some of his stories in Ohio. The "Western" novel has never been successfully defined. West of the Mississippi? The Great Plains? The Rockies? In every list of "25 best westerns" is the novel *Man from Snowy River*, which takes place in Australia. Jack London's are set in Alaska.

A few years ago I was serving as president of Western Writers of America. They had decided on Branson, Missouri, for the annual convention. I received several irate letters from members on the west coast, about the location being "back east." My answer was that Jesse James, surely a part of the West, grew up and operated in that area. A bit farther *south* stands the court of the famous Hangin' Judge Parker.

When the average American thinks of the West, what does he visualize? Cowboys, cattle drives, gunfighters, lawmen, buffalo,

Indian battles, cavalry, wagon trains west. And where did *all* of these events take place? In Kansas.

The whole point of the big cattle drives was to get Texas cattle to the railheads in Kansas. Cowboy boots were invented here. (Well east of the 98th meridian, incidentally.) There were more "Indian Wars" skirmishes by cavalry in Kansas than in any other state. George A. Custer was stationed in Kansas for several years, as commandant of the Smoky Hill Military District. The "Buffalo Soldiers" were based here.

Most of the big name gunslingers and/or lawmen operated here. Wyatt Earp, Bat Masterson, Wild Bill Hickock, Doc Holliday, others.

The "Great Buffalo Hunts" took place largely in Kansas (and south into the Oklahoma and Texas panhandles.) Buffalo Bill Cody made his start and his name here.

The Pony Express and the Butterfield Stage Line originated in Kansas. So did the fictional "Little House on the Prairie" series, which began with Laura Ingalls Wilder's childhood memories in *eastern* Kansas. Let's get serious. Is Kansas "West," or what?

I've taught a class for several years at Emporia State University, usually titled something like "Contemporary Western Fiction." There are always some enrollees who expect the "American Western" to be limited to the shoot-out at high noon at the OK Corral. We talk a lot about the fact that just as no one has ever successfully defined the West, no one has defined the American Western in fiction.

On the final exam, I use a question which really has no answer. I just want to see what they think: *Why* has no one ever defined the "Western?" I get some pretty interesting answers, revolving around the fact that no one can really define the "West."

One of the best answers, a couple of years ago, seemed to really grasp the complexity of the problem: "Because the West isn't a place, it's a direction. Everywhere is west of someplace else."

Maybe that's it. Or maybe it's more than that. Maybe The West isn't a place anyway. It's a state of mind.

See you down the road.

Shoulda Been Here

A few weeks ago I wrote about a short side trip, off the Interstate to the back roads. There was one other idea that emerged from that foray. We stopped to look around Wilson, the "Czech capital of Kansas." It was apparent that a few days before, there had been a major celebration of some sort. There were still signs and banners and window displays which told of a major festival. Our impromptu visit was just a few days late. This was verified by a waitress in the little cafe where we stopped for lunch. "Oh yeah! You shoulda been here."

I got to thinking about that over some delicious Czech pastry and coffee. It had happened to us once that day already. We had stopped at the town of Nicodemus, to find that only a week before, they had had their annual historical festival, celebrating the founding of the town by freed slaves. We couldn't have attended that anyway. We had been somewhere else. Our side trip had evolved only that morning. It was okay, no major disaster.

But, I began to think of other instances. My brother and I once took a trout fishing trip to Missouri. We didn't even get a single fish, not even a bite. "You shoulda been here last week," the guy at the bait shop told us. "They were really bitin'!" Of course, the other side of *that* coin was a few years earlier, when I was working at a bait shop on one of the state lakes. I *was* the guy telling the fishermen who were coming in empty-handed, "You shoulda been here last week."

I guess life is rarely perfect. Weather is a good example. Occasionally we have a day or two, or maybe a stretch of Indian Summer, that's nearly perfect. Then we'll have a day that's too hot, too cold, or wet or dry, and we complain. A lady who once worked for me had a pithy comment for people who were overly complainers. "I'd like to have...(whatever...the winning lottery ticket, etc.)," someone would say.

"Sure," she'd answer. "People in hell would like to have ice water, too."

That would sort of put it in perspective. That's the key, of course. We weren't there last week for the festival or the day the fish were biting. But then, we weren't on the TWA flight to Paris which exploded off New York, either. Probably, there have been many times when we *did* happen to be in luck. There was a fishing trip, maybe, when every cast did result in a strike, or nearly so.

There was the time in New Orleans, when we were just wandering around Old Town and saw a bunch of musicians tuning up on the lawn of a public building. There were a lot of men in dark suits busily cruising the neighborhood. We stopped to watch and listen, and asked someone what was the occasion. The President was coming to town, we were told, and the musicians of Bourbon Street were preparing to welcome him. They were beginning to "jam" while waiting.

As it happened, the President's plane was delayed. For about an hour, we were able to hang out on the corner there, and listen. Imagine, the combined bands of Al Hirt, Pete Fountain, and the other great jazz artists of the world. They were doing their thing just for fun, and for the joy of playing with other great musicians, just hangin' out to pass the time. There's no way we could have bought tickets for a concert like that. There probably never *was* a concert like that, before or since.

I've never stopped to think, before, that for some time after that, the citizens of New Orleans had a real zinger for tourists: "Man, youall shoulda been here yesterday! (last week, last month, last year...) Al Hirt and Pete Fountain and all the others stood right there on that corner and just blew for a couple of hours. It was wonderful!"

It was. That experience was probably more meaningful than seeing the President. See one President, you've seen 'em all. But that was the time when we shoulda been there, and we *were*.

I think it probably evens out, in the long run. You win some, you lose some, and some are rained out.

See you down the road.

Floating the Yellowstone August 1994

I mentioned the Western Writers' convention last week, held in Billings, Montana.

The first evening of the conference, a writer friend approached us with an idea. Why not take a boat trip on the Yellowstone River while we were there? Edna and I are usually ready for such things, (that's well known in the organization) so things developed quickly. There were about a dozen of us. A handful of writers, a New York editor, a couple of young teenagers whose respective parents had entrusted them to us and to others of the party. It really is a family-oriented outfit.

On the Snake River a couple of years ago, we'd taken a float trip on a raft. This was different...A power boat, a jet-propelled craft with only three or four inches of draft. That way, we could arrive at the chosen section of river, the guide would cut the power, and we'd drift. That way we could see about twelve miles of river in a couple of hours one evening.

The guide first took us downstream a couple of miles to show us the shallows where the Crow Indians crossed each autumn to set up winter camp in the sheltered valley. It was easy to visualize the procession. Horsemen, people on foot, pack animals and travois, threading their way across the chain of islands and gravel bars to the flat area on the south side.

Then we started upstream, past the city toward the upper river. There's an old town site which was the upper limit of the river steamboats on the river. Above that point, the Yellowstone is swift, dangerous and unpredictable.

Our guide was good. He knew where to look for beaver, deer, and elk. We saw dozens of white pelicans and other waterfowl.

At one point we came upon two young golden eagles, just learning to fly. The guide shut down the boat and we drifted, watching. One of them struggled in a short flight along the ground, and finally managed to grab a low limb on a pine tree. There, he didn't have the coordination to pull himself upright, so he hung by one leg for a minute or two. Then he let go to drop to the ground and tried again.

We came within a few feet of the biggest beaver lodge I ever saw, some five or six feet tall and even wider across. There were numerous beaver cuttings, mostly among the cottonwoods.

Sandbars with driftwood logs gave the easy impression that the river hasn't changed much in 200 years. We could imagine fur trappers, red or white, crouching behind those logs to defend against attack.

There had been one dark moment earlier. We had seen a number of people along the banks and on a bridge near the town. The guide told us that a search was in progress for a body, a man believed drowned some fifty miles upstream, three days earlier. Our boat had been helping with the search for the first couple of days. He had hardly told us about it when we rounded a bend and encountered a small boat. The two men in the boat were lifting a body out of the water...

By a bizarre twist of fate, it was not the drowning victim from upstream, but another. This was a local teenager who had tried to swim in the treacherous river. We didn't know that until the next day. The really dark part of that story was that the young man's friends had attacked a TV newswoman who was filming the scene. They spat on her, slashed the tires on the news car, and smashed the windows with rocks. The newswoman finally locked herself in the vehicle and radioed for help. In my opinion, there is no tragedy that would justify such behavior on the part of these delinquents. Has everybody gone nuts? The sheriff was considering filing charges when we left.

One more odd coincidence: The guide on our boat and his partner were the ones who found the other body the next day. A pretty tough week for them and their families, I'd guess. And the Yellowstone keeps its reputation for danger and treachery. But it's still a beautiful river.

See you down the road.

Home for the Holidays

December 2001

I've written on this topic before, but not for a number of years. This time, a couple of unrelated factors nudge me toward a revisitation of the topic; warm firesides, family…A sort of warm fuzzy event.

The first of these factors was that of the calendar. A weekly column has to be dated at regular intervals. Obviously, weekly. Years ago I chose Monday. Some subscribing papers are daily papers, and some do use the feature on Mondays. But some of the weekly subscribers publish on Tuesday or Wednesday. No problem, usually. They simply use that week's column. Occasionally, however, this sort of works into a log jam. I didn't realize it until I started to write December's columns. Most columnists use a seasonal theme at least part of the time. To completely ignore the major holidays in a weekly column would be unforgivable. How, then, am I going to write seasonal topics for Christmas and New Year? The dates on the columns will be Christmas Eve and New Year's Eve, but most of the papers using them will publish a couple of days later. Date them a week early? That would, for Monday-published papers, put the New Year's topic on Christmas Eve. (Actually, this would be the publisher's problem, but · they have enough of those without any that I might contribute. I try to be helpful.)

The other factor involved the fact that in October, I managed to really overextend myself with out-of-town commitments. When we returned from the five-day lecture marathon in South Dakota, which I wrote about recently, I received an ultimatum. My long-suffering spouse suggested that I book no more appearances beyond those already on the calendar, until after the holidays. Otherwise, it was hinted, I might return home to find most of my stuff out in the front yard, as in some American Indian cultures. I think she was joking, but I'm taking no chances.

We will spend the holidays at home. Some couples we know will probably travel to exotic foreign locations or take a cruise between Christmas and New Year. We've gone on trips a few times during that week. When one of our daughters was teaching in Brown's Park, Colorado, a few years ago, we'd spend that interim there. It was a real treat to participate in a traditional New Years Eve party in the old Lodore School building, with a couple dozen neighbors from a sixty-mile radius. That's all the people they *have* in the area.

In any thinly-populated area, there is a different feeling, a different attitude toward others. People help each other without hesitation, because they need each other. Their own cultural, religious, and racial backgrounds fade to unimportance in such a setting. There's a feeling of camaraderie which just can't exist in heavily-populated areas. There's no "us" versus "them," just us...*All* of us. In this case, a mix of Greek Orthodox, Protestants, Roman Catholics and Mormons. Nobody saw anything unusual about this mix, because they live it every day. Anyone there would help anyone else in a situation of need.

Everyone brought food, a wonderful ethnic mix. Even though we were outlanders, we were welcomed, too. They had their own band, and danced until dawn, a tradition in the valley. We were told that Butch Cassidy had attended this same party in the same building a generation ago. (The 4-H club in Brown's Park is called "The Wild Bunch.")

We attended that party twice, but on both occasions, on returning home, we felt that somehow we'd *missed* the holidays. Yes, we'd had a tree, we'd had Christmas at home, before we traveled, but it wasn't the same. We decided that we *need* the few days between Christmas and New Year, to sit by our own fire and feel warm and fuzzy and home.

See you down the road.

A Special Day

A few weeks ago, we had the privilege of attending a very special ceremony at Baker University. I graduated from Baker quite a few years ago, and have a warm spot in my heart for my alma mater. In recent years I've been honored to serve on her Board of Trustees. That has led to some interesting situations, but none more impressive than one this past autumn.

Some years back, Mr. Robert Osborne of Olathe conceived the idea of the gift of a chapel for the Baker campus. Baker is the oldest university in Kansas, having been chartered in 1858. It was founded by the Methodist Church, but, oddly, there has never been a place of worship on the University proper. Church services and choir performances have been at the Baldwin City United Methodist Church across the street. Mr. Osborne's idea was for a small, intimate chapel, to be located on the campus itself. He proposed to move an old chapel from England, the place of Methodism's origins, to be reconstructed on the Baker campus.

The story of the discovery of such an abandoned chapel in Sproxton, England, its acquisition, transport, and reconstruction at Baker reads like fiction. The 25,000 stones were marked with numbers as they were removed and packed in sawdust for shipment in some 200 crates, along with the stained glass windows and exquisite woodwork. The pews had been sold, so new pews in the original style were manufactured in Garnett, Kansas, to replace the seating. Meanwhile, reconstruction was in progress on the Baker campus.

Nearly a year ago, the trustees were informed in advance of a very special event. The rededication of the chapel would be enhanced by the participation of Lady Margaret Thatcher, former Prime Minister of Britain. Lady Thatcher was born at Grantham, England, near Sproxton, and her father, a lay Methodist minister, had often preached in this chapel. In addition to the baroness, a party of several members of the church from Grantham and Sproxton attended the ceremonies.

This was a day of major importance in Baldwin City and at the

University. Thousands of people descended on the quiet campus. There was national coverage by the media. Nature contributed to the confusion with a record-breaking earliest snow on the twenty-second of October. The University campus, carefully manicured for this great occasion, was now littered with broken tree branches and snow turning to slush.

It didn't matter. The occasion was too great to be spoiled by such minor nuisances. The "Right Honorable the Baroness Thatcher, LG, OM, FRS," (according to the program) proved to be a charming lady, a really nice person, and a superb speaker. She received applause several times at her lecture, as well as standing ovations.

The rededication itself was outside the chapel, of course. The structure seats barely a hundred people. Lady Thatcher participated in this, too. The rededicated building will be the Clarice L. Osborne Memorial Chapel, in honor of the wife of Mr. Osborne, whose gifts made the whole thing possible.

It was a marvelously colorful ceremony, with hundreds of small American and British flags, waved by school children from the Baldwin elementary school down the street. There was bagpipe music by the St. Andrews Pipes and Drums from Kansas City, who had come to participate in the ceremonies. It was a great day, one which those school children can tell about to their grandchildren. The visiting British church members were charmed and charming in their reactions.

Maybe my best memory of this whole series of events, though, will be a very simple one. When the first crates of stones were arriving from England and being unpacked, we were in Baldwin for a trustees' meeting, curiously looking at the numbered stones. There was one, about the size of a brick, which had no number. Instead, a workman in England had lettered, with the same black marker as the numbers, his own greeting: "Hello, Yanks!"

See you down the road.

The Garden of Eden

September 1996

During our recent trip across the back roads of Kansas, one of our stops was the Garden of Eden at Lucas. We'd heard about it for years, but just never had the opportunity before to turn off the beaten path for a look.

This is one that's hard to describe. In 1907, Samuel P. Dinsmoor, Civil War veteran, moved from Ohio to Lucas and began his astonishing project. He was sixty-four, and wanted to build what he called a Cabin Home on the frontier. He had in mind a log cabin, but was hindered by a factor he had not considered: There were no logs on the Kansas prairie.

Undaunted, Mr. Dinsmoor noted that in that country, fence posts were of stone. He would build his cabin of the same material. Not just stone, but stone *logs*. He rigged his wagon to haul the posts, some twenty feet long, from the sandstone quarry to his building site, in a sling beneath the wagon. He actually notched the ends like logs, and built the house, which is still sturdy and sound, without a crack. The "cabin" has eleven rooms, on three levels, with plastered walls and conventional hardwood trim inside.

Behind the house, he built a mausoleum, of the same stone posts, to be the resting place for himself and his wife, Frances. They had been married on horseback in 1870, and raised five children.

On the very top of the mausoleum was a concrete American flag, which rotated as a weathervane. Its weight was counter-balanced by a concrete turkey. Dinsmoor agreed with Ben Franklin that the turkey, not the eagle, should be the national symbol. The flag and turkey have now been removed to the lawn. The metal swivel was rusting and becoming a threat to visitors below.

It's unsure when he began the construction of the Garden of Eden, which can best be described as concrete yard art on a gigantic scale. The first figures were of Adam and Eve, the serpent, and a concrete apple tree some thirty feet high. It's said that the community rebelled somewhat over Adam's nakedness, so Mr. Dinsmoor, a member of the Masonic Lodge, added a concrete Mason's apron, in lieu of a fig leaf.

It's worth noting that although Dinsmoor wasn't much of an artist, he was a fine workman and craftsman. His reinforced concrete projects are still in pretty good shape after nearly a century.

From there, he added other scenes from scripture, although not exactly as usually translated. I don't recall, for instance, the description of Abel's death in which the body is discovered by Abel's wife and his shepherd dog. The wife and the dog have exactly the same expression on their concrete faces. (A shepherd dog? "Of course," Mr. Dinsmoor insisted. "He was a shepherd, wasn't he? He must have had a dog!")

Another scene shows the banishment of Adam and Eve from the garden, an angel with spread wings, and Satan's glee. All of these and other scenes are high overhead in the concrete trees. There are more than two dozen trees, mostly about thirty feet tall.

At the corner of the block, the concrete scenery changes from religious to political. Dinsmoor was a member of the Populist party. Frankly, the meaning of some of his concrete political cartoons is lost on most people, I think. However, his last work of art, the Crucifixion of Labor, has a meaning that's plain. The laboring man is being impaled by four torturers, who are labeled for sure identification: Politician, Doctor, Lawyer, Banker. He was not quite able to finish this scene before the loss of his eyesight, about 1929.

But along the way Dinsmoor did some other remarkable things, too. He was a skilled woodworker. In the house are several pieces of his furniture, including tables with intricately inlaid tops.

It's hard to see how this man, after retirement age, could have accomplished all of this. There were 113 tons of concrete, (2,273 sacks), all hand mixed, besides the stone house.

Maybe an even greater accomplishment, though, is that in 1924, at the age of 81, he married again, a twenty year old woman, and fathered two more children.

See you down the road.

The House on Wheels

There was a short time, quite a few years ago, when I was a single parent for a year or so. I decided to take a couple of small daughters on a camping trip to Colorado.

I knew the area quite well. I'd been in professional YMCA camping for several years. There was a camp ground in Rocky Mountain National Park where I'd always wanted to take a family vacation, and we headed there, equipped with sleeping bags and cooking equipment. But, I'd been away from camping for five years, in graduate school, and times had changed.

Imagine my surprise, on driving my old station wagon into the camp area, to find it overrun with people. It was literally marked off with white stripes, in numbered squares so small that it looked like a parking lot. People were tripping over the tent ropes of the people in the next square. There were also a large number of "campers" and camping trailers of various sizes and styles, some pretty big. No one could see any scenery because of all the vehicles. It was like camping in the parking lot at the mall, except that there were no malls yet. This, of course, was not camping. It still isn't.

I didn't even stop the car. They had spoiled one of my favorite places. I made a U-turn and drove out. We checked into an economically priced motel in Estes Park, and spent several days driving from there to some of the more remote and unspoiled areas which I wanted to show my kids.

It was a time of transition which is still going on. From tents to campers and camp trailers to motor homes and RVs. (There are still people who enjoy real camping, of course, but this isn't about them.)

A few days ago one of the TV morning news shows had a segment on this subject. They showed vehicles of all sizes, but the object appeared to be to see how big they could be and still get on the highway. Huge vehicles, the size of a boxcar, costing twice what our house cost when we built it. Nearly as big, too. They talked about the freedom of the open road, and all that. Where's the freedom in being saddled with a monster vehicle that takes several parking places, and pulling your car behind it? "We can stop anywhere we like!" one of the women said brightly. Not exactly…There are limited areas where you can park, not even counting the necessary "hookups" if you're staying more than a day or two.

We took a trip with relatives a few years back, in one of these upscale, high-dollar rolling residences. It was one of my more memorable experiences…"All the conveniences"…Right. As convenient as the toilet facilities on an airplane. Why anyone would want to expose themselves to such discomfort, I can't imagine. That's not even counting the fact that they're usually blocking the view of the highway, road signs, and scenery from normal drivers. (I really think it's mostly a "My car's bigger than yours" thing. But what do I know? I drive a pickup truck.)

Cost? Well, of course you don't have to buy one. You can lease or rent. Figures given on the news program have them up to eighty thousand dollars. Lease, at a thousand a week, plus $100 a night in an RV park. Mileage on these monsters, 8 to 10 miles per gallon.

Let's see…We recently returned from a trip to a meeting in Albuquerque. We were gone for a week. If we'd had all the "convenience" of a good motor home…Let's say we rent it at a bargain, only 900 dollars…Plus four nights at a hundred each. (We'll save money by taking up six parking spaces in the hotel parking lot until they ask us to leave.) Mileage, at the top estimate, ten miles per gallon…1600 miles, 160 gallons at $1.30, usually more, at least 200 dollars. Of course, we'd save money on meals. (Well, maybe.)

Back in the real world, we made this trip in our car. We stayed at the Marriott, where the convention was held. Our total cost, with air conditioning, a good shower, king size bed, and all meals, was less than half what we'd have spent in the RV. And we didn't even have to try to jockey a box-car sized rolling barn through Albuquerque traffic. Or, block the view of the mountains for normal people.

See you down the road.

Alaska

It must have been in December that the phone rang...A call from a publicist at Bantam-Doubleday-Dell, my publisher.

After the usual greetings, he got down to the point.

"Would you be willing to take a promotional tour to Alaska?"

Well, that took only a moment to consider. Of course I would... But wait...This promotion would be for a couple of upcoming books, due for release in February and March, 1995...Books are usually available two or three weeks before the official release...January or February...Alaska? Go slow here, Don...

"When did you have in mind?" I asked as casually as I could manage. He laughed. "Oh, not right away! How about June?"

June was already pretty full, with a publicity tour and book signings in southern Missouri, the Tallgrass Writing Workshop at Emporia State, and the annual Western Writers' Convention in El Paso. But how often does a chance like this happen? I quickly checked my pocket calendar. There was a week there in the middle.

"Sure," I said as calmly as I could, "if it could be between these dates." I gave him my schedule.

"That will work," he said agreeably. "Now, if Edna wants to go, I can tell you what her ticket would cost. And, you may want to stay over an extra day or two to see the sights."

I was afraid I'd wake up and find I was dreaming all this. A chance to see Alaska! It's a place we've always wanted to go anyway, but had never felt we could afford it. This way, though, my expenses would be covered, and we'd be responsible only for her plane fare and a few incidentals. Dates would be worked out later, right up to the last day or two as new appearances and book signings were added.

I sauntered casually out to the kitchen to ask Edna if she'd like to go to Alaska with me. I think they almost heard her acceptance in Fairbanks. But pretty soon she returned to earth and began to ask details, which of course we didn't have yet. We'd get those later.

Now to back up a bit, there was a time when I actually considered settling in Alaska. I was just about to be mustered out of the Army, and I happened to pick up a copy of a magazine from Alaska, then Alaska

Territory, before statehood. There was an article about homestead land still available.

It was an intriguing thought. I had no major responsibilities yet. I had just turned twenty. (I would not meet Edna for another ten years, but I didn't know that yet, of course.) The thing that really hooked me was something I hadn't known: Military service could be counted against time necessary to prove out on a homestead, month for month. Not only that, combat time counted double.

Wow! I quickly counted on my fingers...The way it worked out, I'd have considerably more than half my homestead time already served. I requested and received the necessary papers to fill out, along with maps and more detailed requirements. I was narrowing it down to an area on the Kenai Peninsula, where the Japan current warms the southern shores. I was planning what sort of log structure I could build, and making sketches.

I was discharged in August, and arrived home to Kansas about the sixth. I realized that by the time I got to Alaska and filed my homestead claim, it would be too late to start building a place to live. Too expensive to stay there, or to travel back and forth. Travel was almost entirely by ship.

So, I might as well enroll in a semester of college and defer the homestead to next spring, I figured. Then I'd have the summer to begin to build.

Well, the best-laid plans are sometimes diverted. During that first semester of college at Baker University, my hormones began to whisper to me. I realized that there were girls in college, and very few in the Kenai. I had just spent a while in the Pacific and...Well, Alaska would still be there, right?

That was true. It still is there, but I never did get up to see it, until June, 1995. Regrets? Not really. I would never have met Edna...But more Alaska later.

See you down the road.

Land of the Midnight Sun   August 1995

I well remember the chapter on Alaska in my Junior High School Geography book. Its title is unforgettable: "Land of the Midnight Sun." That was a thrilling phrase, hinting at romance and adventure and mystery. Somehow the idea of a place where it's still sunny at midnight captured my imagination. I've always enjoyed long summer evenings and quiet twilight. I didn't completely understand how the midnight sun thing works. (I still don't, but it's because of the seasons and the earth's tilt and all that. In winter, of course, it's dark except for an hour or two about noon.) Even though it's always been fascinating to me, I'd almost completely forgotten to look for it on our recent trip to Alaska.

That was a pretty long day, the first one. Alaska has its own time zone, which makes a three hour difference from Central time. We flew out of Kansas City at 6:30 AM, crossed into Mountain time to stop at Salt Lake City...Then, on to Seattle in the Pacific time zone, a two hour layover and on to Juneau, Alaska, on its own time.

Of course each of those zone changes made it an hour earlier. When we arrived in Juneau, and checked into the hotel, it was only 4:45 PM. However, by our time at home, that's nearly eight o'clock. And, our day had started at 4:30 AM.

But now it was time to go to work. I was scheduled to sign books at a mall bookstore from 6 to 8 PM. (That's 9 to 11 in the time zone where we started the day.)

The thought crossed my mind that it was a strange time of day to have a book signing, but I hadn't really figured it out yet. About the long daylight, that is.

I signed books, visited with customers, and headed back to the hotel about 8:30. (11:30 Central time at home.)

We hadn't eaten since we landed, so stopped in the hotel restaurant to get some nourishment. It was only then that we realized that it really wasn't dark yet, even when we finished eating. By that time it was 10 PM, and the sun was just setting (1 AM at home...We'd had a 20 hour day, and we slept pretty well.)

Farther north in Anchorage, we really saw the difference. The sun sets later and later as we approach the Arctic Circle. At 11 PM, all the downtown shops were still open and the sun just preparing to set.

Another 200 miles north at Fairbanks, we were really impressed. The sun literally did not set until after midnight. We were like kids who hate to go to bed before it gets dark. We were afraid we'd miss something.

There really were things going on, too. While we were in Fairbanks, there was the occasion of an annual run to raise money for deprived children, or some similar worthy cause. There was an impressive amount of advertising promotion about it. The starting time: 10 PM! One of the runners straggled past our hotel about midnight, and the sun wasn't completely down yet.

Does it get completely dark at all, dark enough to see the stars? Well, yes. Somewhere between 1 and 3 AM, for an hour or so, apparently. And, we were there within a day or two of the summer solstice, the longest day of the year, which made the dark part the shortest.

We'd start to get ready for bed, draw the drapes and all, but then there was a temptation to look outside one more time. There might be something interesting going on.

On our last night in Alaska, it was that way. We'd have an early plane to catch, so had done all but our last minute packing. Edna pulled back the drape for one last peek. It was just midnight, and the sun was a thin sliver of fire through the trees. She gave a pleasant little gasp of surprise and pointed off to the south. (I guess it was south. Directions are hard to figure when the sun rises and sets in the same general area.)

Anyway, there we stood, at midnight, watching a beautiful sunset. As an extra added attraction, someone was launching a colorful hot air balloon about a mile away. I remembered a line from one of Robert Service's poems about the Yukon. "There are strange things done in the midnight sun…"

I'll be telling about some more of them in the coming weeks.

See you down the road.

The Ice Lady July 1996

Last year, we had the opportunity to go to Alaska on a book promotion tour. There was a bit of extra time, and we had a company rental car at our disposal. This was a wonderful opportunity to see and do some things not available on the average package tour to Alaska.

Some of the things we found most fascinating were the glaciers. I had always thought that a glacier, being formed by hard-packed snow, would look like a snow field. Yes, it does look somewhat like that, but it's a different color. But isn't white *white*? Not really...

Our first look at a glacier was as we flew into Juneau. The plane banked into a turn, and there below us was a glacier, bright luminous blue, in sharp contrast to the snowy mountains we'd been crossing. The blue color, we learned, is because glacial ice has an entirely different crystalline structure than any other ice or snow anywhere on earth. It has been subjected to not only cold, but pressure, as well as time. Some glaciers are miles thick, and the weight of the centuries of ice and snow piling up on top of previous centuries causes a crystal of different structure. This alters the refraction of light so that the glacial ice appears blue.

One of the appealing things to me was the thought of the ancient status of the ice that we could see and touch. Some of it, millions of years old. There was a strange, otherworldly feeling about it, like reading a science-fiction or fantasy novel, except that it's here and it's real. This was made more impressive by the knowledge that there are creatures that live inside that ice..."Ice worms" which burrow in the glacier itself. You can see their little tunnels.

Ice, though it's pretty solid, acts like a very slow liquid. A glacier can be visualized as a river, flowing downslope toward the sea. It takes centuries to do it. There, it will break off in chunks to become icebergs. Sometimes, though, this ancient ice melts just a little faster than it moves. In that case, the face of the glacier at the lower end is on land. Instead of becoming icebergs in the ocean, it becomes melting ice that we can see and touch and walk on.

There are also some strange things which come out of the melting ice of these glaciers. Creatures which have been trapped in a sudden climate change, or fallen into a crevice in the surface of the ice field. Hairy elephants, some nearly intact. Some of them were frozen so rapidly that the stomach contents from their last meal can be identified. That must have been a tremendously major event on planet earth! Early explorers in Siberia fed their sled dogs on some of the frozen meat of these mammoths.

A few years ago the corpse of a man who lived thousands of years ago thawed from a European glacier, providing fascinating information on early humans. He was referred to in the press as the Ice Man.

At one of the glaciers we visited, people were walking and climbing around on the surface of the ice. It looked a little dangerous. While we watched the adventurous, we spoke and visited with other tourists. Several women admired the blanket jacket Edna was wearing, one with bright southwest designs.

I asked her whether she'd like to go out on the ice a little way, just to say we did. She declined. She'd probably fall into one of the deep crevices, she said, and melt out in a couple of thousand years.

"They could call me the Ice Lady, I guess," she joked. "They'd study my frozen body, and then somebody would probably say 'Too bad...But she was sure wearing a cute jacket, wasn't she?'"

See you down the road.

The Steamboat Arabia June 1996

Not long ago I was working on a story in which part of the action takes place on a river steamer. If you examine the Great Seal of the State of Kansas, you'll notice that one of the most prominent features is a packet steamboat.

These specially designed "prairie steamers" traveled the Missouri and the Kansas Rivers regularly. Until the coming of the railroads, this was the massive transportation system which moved passengers and freight to the opening West.

I needed to find a bit more information on the industry, and decided to visit the Arabia Steamboat Museum in Kansas City. I'd heard and read about it, and knew some of the background.

It was a risky industry, with shifting sandbars and floating tree trunks and snags that could rip the hull of a steamboat. It is estimated that there are at least 300 sunken steamboats between St. Louis and Kansas City alone. Some lie at the bottom of the rivers. Others, like the *Arabia*, are buried beneath the silt, as the river changes its course.

The "Great White *Arabia*," 188 feet in length, had been operating on the Missouri for only three years when her end came. She carried 130 passengers and some 200 tons of freight, bound for the frontier cities of Nebraska and Iowa. Many of the passengers were women and children, en route to join their husbands and fathers.

On September 5, 1856, the *Arabia* struck a jagged sycamore snag at Quindaro Bend, less than an hour out of Kansas City. In ten minutes she lay at the bottom. The river was shallow, so for a time the upper decks were above water. This enabled the escape of all passengers and crew, either swimming or transported to shore by the one lifeboat. The only casualty was the carpenter's mule, tied on the aft lower deck.

In a few days the *Arabia* had settled into the soft mud of the Missouri's bed, not to be seen for 130 years.

There have always been rumors about the richness of her cargo. News stories of the time speculated about everything from gold to "400 barrels of Kentucky bourbon," a valuable commodity. Three attempts at salvage, in 1877, 1897, and 1974, met with limited success.

In 1988, River Salvage, Inc., of Independence, Missouri, tackled the task. It was a family project; David Hawley and his father Bob, brother Dave, and a couple of friends, David Lutrell and Jerry Mackey. They located the wreck, deep under Norman Sortor's soybean field, half a mile from the river's present channel, using metal detectors. Core drillings verified that it was indeed the boat.

The story of the excavation itself reads like a novel, but within a few weeks they had begun to reach the cargo. Not gold or bourbon, but a full load of another sort of treasure. Cargo, headed for the frontier. Two hundred tons of it, the largest collection of pre-Civil War artifacts in the world. Originally it had been planned to sell the artifacts, but it became apparent that it was more important from an archaeological viewpoint. Hence, the Museum of the Steamboat *Arabia*, in the Old Market area of Kansas City.

I've seen a lot of museums, but this has to be one of the finest anywhere. You can see the size and shape of the boat, her boilers and engines, the restored paddle wheel and drive shaft, and most importantly, the cargo. Everyday items for use on the frontier. Canned goods in glass jars...Pickles, still edible. Boots and shoes, mostly "straight last." Right and left weren't yet in common use. Likewise, lamps for settlers' homes, designed for whale oil, because kerosene wouldn't come until later. Many candles, still usable, as well as wooden boxes of matches with which to light them. (The matches aren't usable, of course.)

There are broad-brimmed beaver hats, ladies' and children's clothing, and hundreds of bolts of yard goods, from silks to ginghams. French perfume, well preserved and with fragrance intact. Of major interest are the tools. Some are unfamiliar, others nearly like those in the hardware store today.

It's a real education, as well as fun. Hours are 10-6 Monday to Saturday, noon to five Sunday. Admission fees are reasonable.

See you down the road.

The
Human Condition

Environmental Education

November 1994

In September a special dedication took place at the Wolf Creek Nuclear Energy site. In the 1970s land was acquired in Coffey County for the construction of the Wolf Creek nuclear plant. Like any other form of electrical generating system, there were several basic needs. There must be a pond or lake of about 5,000 acres to provide water to cool the giant turbines which generate the electricity. This was created by impounding a section of Wolf Creek. Such a lake, of course, is irregular in shape and is surrounded by some 5,000 more acres of farm and ranch land.

The generating plant only occupies about 300 acres, and the rest continues to be used as it always has been. About two-thirds is grassland, leased for grazing. The cropland is still farmed, too, by many of the people who farmed it before the nuclear plant, on lease or shares.

There are a lot of different problems in a sizable lake, grasslands, croplands, and woodlands, interacting with the power plant's operation. The lake alone, for instance...It will be a few degrees warmer in winter than other bodies of water in the area. There must be a careful balance of predator fish to scavengers, different from the average pond. The quality of the runoff from grass and cropland is important. To manage all of this, the operating corporation employs a number of biologists. They operate out of a building along the approach to the power plant, called the Eisenhower Educational Center. Biologists from other parts of the world study the fish management program at Wolf Creek.

There are some side benefits. Because of the warm outflow basin, fish congregate and remain more active through the winter. This in turn encourages eagles to winter there, and at least one pair has nested at the lake. It's a favorite wintering area for waterfowl, too.

It was only a matter of time until these biologists began to see other possibilities. Why not a series of nature trails, open to the public, and geared to tours by school classes? There are at least three different ecological areas available: Grasslands, woodlands, wetlands, plus the lake itself. When the idea was announced, people began to offer help. Boy Scout troops and individuals built trails and bridges. 4-H clubs erected rest benches. Coffey County donated recycled asphalt to make the foot trails handicap accessible. Employees of the power plant and the operating company donated time, labor, and expertise. Ducks Unlimited and Quail Unlimited, outdoor sportsmen's organizations who virtually invented wildlife conservation, got involved, along with the Kansas and U.S. Wildlife Departments.

The dedication took place September 20, 1994, at the new Wolf Creek Environmental Education Area. There are three foot trails with markers and a brochure which enables a self-guided tour. The Prairie Lake Trail and the South Pond Trail are hard-surfaced, and are fairly short circles, perhaps half a mile, with benches to pause for a rest if needed. The Kansas Nature Trail is a bit longer, maybe a mile. All of these start and end at an old silo on the original Phillips farmstead. The present Educational Area is 160 acres, but expansion to some 500 acres is in the works.

There's a lot to see already. Wild turkeys, deer, assorted small mammals, waterfowl, and plants. Signs furnish directions and suggestions, and are coordinated with the brochures. These brochures, incidentally, are seasonal, because a different set of flowers, grasses, migratory birds, etc., are seen at different times of the year.

There are such amenities as rest rooms, which are handicap accessible. The bird viewing blind on the Prairie Lake Trail is, also. It's a wonderful facility, big enough to hold a classroom of students. There are special facilities for photographers, and the glass windows are slanted to eliminate glare and to allow the waterfowl to come right up to arm's length, without the viewer being seen.

The best part is that all of this will be available to the public, without charge. The location is just off Highway 75, north of Burlington.

See you down the road.

A Guy Thing

When a customer goes through the check out at Bluestem Farm and Ranch Supply in Emporia, the ladies at the cash registers ask politely if there's anything else. Well, usually there is, but I'll think of it later, after I'm nearly home, or when I'm out at the pasture.

I stopped at the feed store the other day to pick up a few sacks of range cubes for the cattle. That saves a lot of cowboying. It's handy to have cattle come to you, just to see if you brought any cubes, even in summer. A lot easier than trying to catch them. Anyway, Harry asked me the same question…Anything else? I mentioned the way I handle that question at Bluestem. Also, that Edna insists that I have withdrawal symptoms if I don't have occasion to go to Bluestem every day or two. Harry allowed that there are a lot of guys like that.

"Well, that's a guy thing," said Virginia, looking up from her work at the computer. "Guys need a place like Bluestem."

Harry and I agreed. Very quickly, we had identified a number of guy things, which are gender-specific, and which most women aren't likely to understand…TV remote controls, and surfing the channels…Duct tape…(Now there's a heavy one…What did guys have before duct tape? Baling wire, probably, but what before *that*? Rawhide, maybe? It boggles the mind, how much older technology has been lost by the encroachment of science and industry. It's sort of sad…Nostalgia just ain't what it used to be. But, I digress…)

Unwillingness to stop for directions if you're traveling…(Yes, we're all guilty of that one.) Leaving the toilet seat up, Virginia suggested. Now I never had much trouble with that. You don't spend many years in a house with six women, a wife and five daughters, without realizing that it's counterproductive to leave toilet seats up. Something a guy just doesn't do.

Now, it goes without saying that there are girl things which guys will never understand, too. For instance, when he asks what's the matter, and she meets the inquiry with one of two answers: a) Stony silence, or b) "If you don't know, I'm not going to tell you!"

In this situation, the best course of action is to go somewhere out of sight and ponder what might have been your infraction which initiated such behavior. (Maybe the toilet seat...)

Another girl thing is shopping. I've written about that before. If a guy needs some small item, he goes to the store and buys it. (Probably at Bluestem.) It requires only a few moments. A woman, on the other hand, is encumbered by all sorts of rules when she goes to buy something. She must look at the item in a prescribed number of stores before the purchase. (A minimum of three, apparently, though a mere man is incapable of even understanding the rules.) The final fourth-quarter move is back to the first store.

As I was writing this, trying to figure out how to avoid offending female readers, the phone rang. It was a male friend, who asked if we'd like to come over for an impromptu fish fry on the following evening. It sounded like a good idea, and I checked my pocket date book...All clear.

I figured I'd better clear it with Edna, though. I hollered at her, and she said fine, sounds like fun. Our friend on the phone said okay, we'll let the girls finalize and confirm the arrangements. His wife was at hand, so I called to Edna again. She was busy, and suggested that the two guys go ahead, make and confirm the details.

I relayed the information, and the gender gap began to widen. No way, he said, that he'd be a party to making and confirming such a thing. Well, I felt nearly the same way. I was glad of the excuse to say something like, "Me too, they'll have to do it."

There are just some things that are guy things, some are girl things. Despite all the denial and the efforts to unisex everything, there *are* differences in gender. For which, let us give thanks.

See you down the road.

Women's Work

I was talking on the phone recently to a friend in another part of the country. She's a young career woman, in marketing and sales, and we met a few years ago as a result of the fact that she was traveling and selling my books.

Since then she has married, and we attended her wedding. Somewhat over a year ago, our friend had her first child, and immediately went back to work. She's still with the same publisher, but in a somewhat different, non-traveling job, which suits her new family status well. We still work together sometimes for book signings and publicity tours.

That's what we were discussing recently. In the course of the conversation I asked about the family, and she told me they're all fine, the baby growing and walking, and all the fun things that yearling babies do. Then she commented on what a different life style she has now. Anyone who ever raised a child knows about that. But she summed it up so beautifully, in one sentence, based around her magazine subscriptions: "I used to take *Cosmopolitan* and *Glamour*...Now it's *Parents* and *Good Housekeeping*."

Well, most of us have been there. It does make a difference when a baby arrives in a family. However, this started me thinking about how job descriptions have changed for women. Having raised five girls, I've been quite aware of this. Once when our youngest was the only one still at home, I showed her one of my favorite books from my own teenage years. It's the *How-to Book for Boys*. It had a great many fun projects, such as kites and wagons and costumes and outdoor games and camping hints. Fun things.

To my astonishment, our daughter wasn't intrigued, but indignant. "Huh! For *boys*!" I protested that there was probably one for girls, too. "Sure," she agreed. "All about how to sew and cook and clean house!"

She had me cornered, there. She was right. A woman's job description was to learn to take care of a house, kitchen, and family. A man's, to go out and create and build and farm and earn the living.

Times change. Young women are able to compete for almost any job now. In most young couples, both work outside the home. Granted, there are inequities, but our culture has come a long way. I well remember the first couple we knew who moved depending on *her* job, not his. She was highly educated and had better job opportunities, so it made sense. But that was thirty years ago, and they were considered a little strange. Now, it's not that unusual. Young men often take a bigger part in caring for babies, too. Once, all diaper-changing in public restrooms happened in the women's facility. There was a question of how old a small boy should be before his mother stops taking him into the ladies' restroom. Now, many men's restrooms have diaper-changing tables and equipment.

I think all this is good, part of the trend for women to become other than second class citizens. They certainly were. When I was born, my mother had been able to vote in a national election only twice, because women couldn't vote until then.

My brother once said that the feminist movement was started by Vincent Bendix. Jim's theory was that women couldn't escape from female bondage because they had no access to transportation. To go anywhere required catching a horse (or team), harnessing, and driving. Many women were not able physically to throw a heavy set of harness up and over the horse's back. She needed a man to help her escape, and if she had one, she was a woman of loose morals. She couldn't win. A few were strong enough, physically and/or emotionally, to accomplish it, but they were rejected by society. Even early cars had to be started with a crank, which was hard work, and often resulted in broken wrists when the engine "kicked." Then came Vincent Bendix with his invention, a device to start the family car...A self-starter. Women began to drive, and now it became easier to escape an abusive relationship. There are still some problems, made more apparent now by those who do effect an escape. Still room for improvement, but we've come a long way, baby.

See you down the road. **DC** ⌣

Good Guys and Bad Guys   June 1996

This past spring we were shocked by the killing of a police officer in Topeka, in a drug raid. There was no question as to who did it. The drug dealer was arrested and tried and found guilty. He admitted that he fired the fatal shot. But the shocker to me, to everybody, I think, was that he was found guilty of a series of lesser crimes. Not first or second degree murder...Possession of drugs, intent to sell, not having a tax stamp, and oh, yes, manslaughter, which carries a minimal jail sentence.

At the time I write this, the sentence has not yet been pronounced. However, it is my impression that if this convicted killer receives the maximum penalty for all his crimes, to run end to end, his longest possible sentence is about eight years. He'll probably be on the street in four years, with time off for "good behavior." Does anybody out there see anything wrong with this picture? We all know of cases where an unquestionably guilty person goes free because of a minor clerical error. Or, because professional jury selectors have stacked a jury with people they know will acquit. If our justice system isn't broken, it is surely badly bent. A few years ago I was testifying in a case, and was appalled at some of the process. "That isn't right!" I remarked to one of the attorneys. He explained it to me, as one would do a child: "Don, it has nothing to do with right and wrong. *This is a court of law.*" I found that a little scary. In my ignorance, I thought that was what the court system was about.

That and justice. Did you ever notice that the emblem of justice, the lady holding the scales, wears a blindfold? Originally, I guess that was so she could balance the facts fairly. Now, it may be so she doesn't become nauseated at the sight of what's going on. (Presumably, she wears ear plugs, too.)

Sometimes it seems that the deck is stacked against the good guys. Sure, the accused is innocent until proven guilty, but how far can you go? Surely the victims have as much right to justice as the criminal. (What does he care? He knows they're not going to do much to him anyway. It's a game.)

But even in a game, there should be ground rules which are fair to both sides. I once heard a standup comedian deal with this subject. Ground rules haven't always been fair in conflicts through history, he pointed out. He wasn't putting it in terms of good guys versus bad guys, but just pointing out what the referee might have said in some of the more well-known historical events.

"Okay, now: The British team has to wear red jackets and march in the open in straight lines. The colonials can hide behind trees and shoot whenever they want to...

"Col. Custer, your cavalry can pick a hill in the open to fire from. The Sioux and Cheyenne will ride round and round while they take turns shooting at you...

"Daltons, you have to rob two Coffeyville banks at the same time and then make a run for it down the alley. Townsmen, you can get guns at the hardware store and shoot the length of the alley from there...

"Black Kettle, your Cheyennes have to camp in the assigned area at Sand Creek. Col. Chivington will attack your women and children at dawn...

"Christians, you wait here in the arena. Romans, you turn the lions loose when the Emperor gives the signal..."

Okay, the rules have never been really fair, and it has seldom had anything to do with right and wrong, historically speaking. But how far can we let it go? I think one problem is that we have never really decided what we want to accomplish in criminal justice. There are at least three possible goals: 1) Punishment 2) Protection for the public, and 3) Rehabilitation.

Let's accept that these three are actually incompatible. Number 2, Protection, is obviously a complete failure. Number 3, Rehabilitation, has been the main thrust for some time now, and is successful in a small minority of cases. To the average criminal, it's only a joke, like the frivolous lawsuits he files to while away the leisure time while he waits to get back on the street.

Isn't it time to take another look at good guys versus bad guys?

See you down the road.

Taking in Laundry May 1996

Another class of college graduates will soon be leaving campuses around the country. It is to be hoped that most of them have jobs, or good possibilities. In this election year, we'll be hearing a lot about what's right or wrong with the country, and part of it will revolve around this ever-present subject. Candidates will be arguing about whose social theories will "create" more jobs.

Somehow, I never figured that a job is something that can be created. It's something that needs to be done, and somebody does it, for which he or she is paid. That's the whole idea of working for pay. But in the last generation or so, this idea has become distorted. There are a lot of people who seem to believe that someone, usually the "Government" owes everybody a living. Everyone "deserves" a living, which includes the guarantee of a job.

I don't see it that way at all. I never believed that anybody deserves anything except what he or she earns. The American work ethic...What happened to it?

A few months ago, the Congress and the President were fighting over the budget. They were like little kids in a sand box arguing over a toy. Except, the toy involved was the United States. Both children were threatening to destroy the toy if they couldn't make the rules about how to play with it. As a result, the Government closed down for a short while a couple of times. We were assured, however, that a skeleton force of "essential" government employees, maybe one in ten, could remain on the job.

Now there's a chilling thought. If only a small percentage of government employees are essential, why in God's name are we paying the rest?

That in turn got me to wondering how many jobs over all are essential in our present economy. Somewhere, there's a balance, an elusive relationship between goods and services. Ultimately, the idea of a job is to do something that needs to be done...Production. Does an effort produce something somebody can use? Against that standard, how many of the country's jobs are actually productive?

Sometimes, they seem anti-productive. We spent nearly a year watching a murder trial in Los Angeles last year. I've heard several estimates of how many millions of dollars were expended by both sides in the O.J. Simpson trial. These dollars really produced nothing except contempt for the injustice of the justice system.

A few years ago, there was a tongue in cheek story about a group of survivors from the sinking of a passenger ship. They managed to make it to a deserted island, as in the Gilligan's Island TV series. But there was nothing there to eat.

Yet, a year later when they were found, all were healthy and in good condition. In amazement, TV newspersons asked how they had managed to survive.

"Easy," said the spokesman for the survivors. "We held a meeting, realized we had a problem, and held an election."

"But there was nothing to eat," protested the interviewer.

"True. But we found that we could all make a living by taking in each others' laundry."

Maybe we missed something along the way. In the intricate balance of goods and services, did we fail to notice that we can't really base an economy on creating services for which there was really no demand?

Are we trying to run the country by taking in each others' laundry?

See you down the road.

The Warrenty Sensor February 1996

There was a time when I could repair my own car. Most kids did work on their first car. We had to, because our first cars were old and in need of repair. Those were the only cars we could afford. But the important thing was, we *could* work on them, because they were well designed, mechanically simple.

The parts that might need attention were also easily accessible. I don't mean *available*. I mean that it was possible to find, reach, and handle nearly everything under the hood. My first car, a 1936 Chevy, could practically be rebuilt with only two or three wrenches.

By contrast, today's models require at least two complete sets of wrenches. One standard, the other metric. ("Metric" is what Japan did to us in revenge for our using the atom bomb.) There are all sorts of special one-purpose tools, too, for all the odd-shaped gadgets. Without these, you can't even change a tire.

And easy to work on? Forget it. There's a rule of some sort now, I think. Every bit of space under a hood must be filled with odds and ends of machinery. Tubes, hoses, wires, tanks, (one for windshield wiper fluid, another for possible overflow from the radiator, etc.), switches, lights…One thing's simpler: There's only one belt, which runs everything. However, when it breaks, *everything* is disabled, and you're sitting beside the road in a dead car.

But back to working on it: I recently watched a mechanic trying to reach one of the simple, frequently-serviced areas under a hood. He was entirely inside the engine compartment, where there's no room anyway. Both feet in the air, trying to reach the parts he needed…That thing was designed, I reasoned, to be repaired only by a left-handed midget, standing on his head.

The thing that really makes it tough on a shade-tree mechanic, however, is that everything has become more and more high-tech. An auto repair shop needs more electronic gadgetry than a doctor's office. It's hard to *tell* what's wrong with the engine without all of this equipment. The car has a lot of it built in, in the form of computer chips and sensors. The car itself is supposed to diagnose what it needs *and* correct it. That's fine, except that it adds another layer of things to go wrong. Because, there's always the possibility of faulty *sensors*. So, if your car tells you there's too much or too little of fuel or air or water or oil, it may be true or not. There's always the possibility that the sensor itself is faulty and needs replacing. Or it may simply be lying. I don't trust machines that are smarter than I am.

How did I happen to be thinking about all this? I'm driving a pickup with 60,000 miles on it, and it's had a few problems. No big ones… An alternator destructed, thirty miles from the nearest shop. I phoned and had a daughter and son-in-law bring one out, and we replaced it beside the road. A fuel filter…Water pump…Battery…Things like that are expected. There was no warranty left on any of this, of course.

This led to another line of thought. Ever notice that when a vehicle breaks down and a part needs to be replaced, the warranty has always expired? Sometimes, just a few days or weeks ago. How does it *know*?

This leads me to a theory which may be a real breakthrough. Maybe as important, even, as the discovery that new automotive finishes attract runaway shopping carts magnetically. Possibly this is unknown even to the manufacturers. But I think that somewhere, hidden in the maze of wires and tubes and hoses and switches in each new vehicle, is one more sensor. The Warranty Sensor.

It is programmed in advance, and lies there waiting. It is activated by the passage of time, perhaps, although that seems too simple. But, whatever initiates it, the action begins immediately. This sensor is interconnected with not only every other sensor, but with every part in the vehicle. It whispers its message, the one signal for which it exists, and things begin to happen. The message is simple, but easily recognizable from the behavior of the vehicle: *The warranty has expired*!

See you down the road.

Rosa Guerrero   September 1995

I was prepared to be unimpressed. Another interpretive dancer... We were at one of the luncheon meetings during the annual convention of Western Writers of America, in El Paso. But by the time Rosa Guerrero had finished her program, I realized that here was a very special person. Smart, pretty, gifted, a marvelous interpreter not only of dance but of life. She lectured as she danced, demonstrating the richness of America's heritage.

I was impressed, too, by a printed flier which had been placed on each table, explaining her program and its philosophy. I spoke to her afterward, and received permission to use it. I don't usually use the writing of others, but this is special. Here are selected thoughts from Rosa Guerrero's "Our Multicultural Tapestry."

*   *   *

Our country is a multicultural tapestry, a mosaic of many people. Each group that represents our land is unique and different. Because of our differentness, we can all contribute something important to the fabric of the American Life. Therefore, each person is special and unequaled.

When God created the earth, He also created a diversified spectrum of birds, flowers, rainbows, and human beings. Thank God for all the differentness. How dull it would be if all of us were the same.

Our traditional folkways are beautiful yet different. We must try to respect the differentness of others. In our culture, with our languages, customs, and values we can demonstrate to the world our diversified folkways.

But what is an American? Is he not a combination of many beautiful cultural groups that make up a tapestry? As a former educator for the El Paso Public Schools for 20 years, I have told my students how beautiful they are. Whether they are black, brown, or white, they are special. In the classroom or during my cultural dance presentations, I have tried to show my students that we are all part of a great cultural flow. We are all Americans who, because of our cultural heritage, contribute something unique to the fabric of American life. We are threads that are woven into a multicultural Tapestry, the fabric of American life. We are like the notes in a chord of music...if all the notes were the same there would be no harmony...no real beauty...because harmony is based on differences, not similarities. This is as true in human relations as it is in music. So I try to teach my students how we can be proud of our differences...how to respect the differentness of others. This...to me...is what my country is all about.

You are Special, you are so very Special. You are different, so great and unique. Look around you...no one in the world is like you. That is why you are so outstanding and so very unique.

Be proud of yourselves, of your culture and heritage. Develop a strong, healthy identity. Never be ashamed of who you are, but strive every day to be a better person. Each day could be your last one, there might not be a tomorrow. All of us have time...how you use it is up to you. Use it wisely, for we are all on borrowed time.

Be positive every day.

If you think you are beaten, you are.

If you think you dare not, you don't.

If you like to win, but you can't, it is almost certain you won't.

If you think you'll lose, you're lost.

For out in the world we find, Success begins with a person's mind.

If you think you are outclassed, you are.

You've got to be sure of yourself before you can ever win a prize.

Life's battles don't always go to the stronger or faster human, but sooner or later the person who wins, is the person WHO THINKS HE CAN!

*   *   *

Thank you, Rosa.
See you down the road.

Mountain Windsong December 1994

A couple of months ago we were privileged to attend a unique event in Norman, Oklahoma. It was the first performance of selections from an upcoming musical, "Mountain Windsong."

Let me back up a few years, though. Robert Conley, a Cherokee author and a friend, was telling me about a novel that he was writing. It was a sort of Cherokee "Evangeline," he said. I remembered Evangeline because I had to read it in Junior High literature class. It's a tragic story of young lovers, separated by the relocation of the French Arcadians from Canada to Louisiana. (The Arcadians became the "'Cajuns," but that's another story.)

I expressed the hope that the Cherokee lovers, separated by a similar relocation via the Trail of Tears, would have better luck than the Arcadians in Evangeline. Conley said he hoped so, too.

This story is built around a Cherokee legend of such a couple, commemorated in a ballad written and sung by Don Grooms, a Cherokee/Creek musician. Its title, "Whippoorwill," the name of the young man. Conley had heard Grooms' ballad, which inspired him to write the novel, *Mountain Windsong*. (University of Oklahoma Press.)

The novel depicts an old man, in modern times, telling his grandson about the people in the legend of Whippoorwill. It's very skillfully done, with a mix of flashbacks and modern-day instructions in the old ways to the boy. The story of the relocation of the Civilized Tribes is retold without the bitterness that might be expected. Certainly, a lot more objectively than I could have done it. But Conley is an award winning best-seller.

Mountain Windsong was well received, and will continue to attract some attention. University presses usually don't even publish fiction, but his is an exceptional story, one of Conley's best works.

Among those who were impressed by it was an internationally known opera singer, Barbara McAlister, also Cherokee. She envisioned the story as a musical, a stage play. From that point it begins to look like a sort of miracle, the way this project has come together. (That story itself could be a movie or stage play.) Robert Conley, who also has experience in the dramatic arts, agreed to write a script based on his novel.

The composer selected for the project is Linder Chlarson, a New York writer of operas, musicals, song cycles, and lyrics. Chlarson is the only person involved in the *Mountain Windsong* project who is not of Indian descent. I had the strong impression from talking to him, though, that he is, in spirit.

He moved to Tahlequah, the Cherokee Nation's capitol, and worked with the Conleys for several weeks. Chlarson wrote the music, and collaborated with Conley on the lyrics.

This first performance, in Norman, Oklahoma, was magnificent. It took place in a building known as the Chouse, an old church with high arched ceilings and stained glass and carved woodwork. The acoustics are wonderful, and the voices well suited to the play and the place.

Barbara McAlister herself sang the alto part, that of Qualla, mother of the main female character, Oconeechee. Her voice was so powerful to hear in that setting, it would almost create an interest in opera.

Oconeechee was played by Alice King, a soprano of Creek descent, a talented young woman who has degrees in both music and psychology, and is a former Miss Creek Nation Princess.

The tenor part of Waguli, "Whippoorwill," was sung by John Moore, another Cherokee with extensive experience in theatre as an actor and vocalist. This past summer he has performed with the Lyric Theatre of Oklahoma.

The father of Oconeechee is Junaluska, played and sung by George W. Stevenson of Choctaw heritage, a man of vast experience in performing and teaching. He is currently on the music faculty at Oral Roberts University.

The pianist for this performance was Timothy Long, of Creek descent, an accomplished concert pianist of national repute.

We were certainly impressed by this sneak preview of some of the numbers in the musical *Mountain Windsong*. It is expected to premiere next summer, probably in Tahlequah. Then who knows? Off-Broadway, Broadway? The writing, the musical score, the performers…This may be a show to watch for.

See you down the road.

"I Never Made a Mistake"   October 1994

A friend startled me a while back with a statement that he had never made a mistake in his life.

I've known people like that, who really believe that they're so superior that they couldn't possibly make any mistakes. I was puzzled, though. This friend is not that sort. He's actually quite humble. And, I could think of a few episodes from his past that would seem to indicate a lapse of good judgment occasionally. For one thing, he had an unfortunate first marriage that ended in disaster. He's never talked much about that one. Then there was a time when he spent a night in jail some thirty years ago because of a youthful prank. Surely that could be classed as a mistake.

For sure, I knew that I've made some mistakes. Really dumb things, usually when I was thinking about something else instead of paying attention to what I was doing. And, I had an unfortunate first marriage myself.

I've changed jobs many times in my life. But wait…That wasn't because I had the previous one by mistake, was it? And didn't I learn from every job? My Army experience, my five years in group work and outdoor recreation as a YMCA director…All the short term things I did along the line…A year as a clergyman (well, they knew I wasn't a real preacher when they hired me.) My mail-order gunsmithing business, my job as a taxidermist, my stint as a vocalist in a quartet. I sold bait in a marina at a state lake one summer. (I had a degree in psychology at the time. Of course, I carefully concealed that fact from the guys at the marina.)

But I'd never thought of any of these as mistakes. These things were just things I did as I went along. All were experiences which have affected my life.

Knowing my friend pretty well, I began to suspect that he had a point to make with his outlandish statement that he'd never made a mistake. I leaned back to hear the rest of it.

This individual has worked at nearly as many things as I have.

He's been a teacher, an actor, a college professor, a writer of good fiction, poetry, and plays. He's also written some pulp fiction under a pseudonym. (The kind you wouldn't want accredited to your own name. A mistake? No, it put groceries on the table during hard times.)

I thought I saw a pattern here. Especially, when I considered his American Indian background. He's something of a philosopher, and the Native philosophies lean heavily toward there being a plan or purpose in all things. I was beginning to see his point, though not completely yet.

"Think about it," he said. "I'm doing work that I love, I just bought a house that I've wanted for years. I have a wonderful wife, children, a grandchild...Now, my world would be different if I'd done things differently, right?"

I had to admit that this seems true, so I nodded.

"Okay," he went on, "So, I wouldn't want anything to be different. Therefore, I must have been making all the right decisions. If I'd ever made a mistake, it wouldn't be like it is. Things would be different. So I guess I've never made any mistakes, have I?"

Well, I had to admit that he had a point there. I applied it to my own life. If anyone had told me a few years ago that I'd have a career doing what I'm doing now, I wouldn't have believed it. (Sometimes I still don't.)

So, in a strange way, maybe I never made a mistake, either, in the sense that our friend means. I'm doing work that I enjoy, working with people I like. I have a great marriage, to my best friend, for the past 34 years. We have five wonderful daughters and six grandchildren.

Some of these we wouldn't have if it hadn't been for that early marriage...Could that have been a mistake, then? Well, it's something to think about, isn't it?

See you down the road.

Wedding Prayer June 1994

June is traditionally a month of weddings. I guess there are several reasons.

In our culture it's the end of a school year. Consequently, a lot of people are finishing their education and moving on to something else. A job, more education, whatever. Graduation..."Commencement."

I used to wonder about that word. "Commence" is a sort of old-fashioned word now, but it formerly was used pretty commonly. It meant to begin something. I couldn't understand why the term was used to signify that you'd just finished something.

I quickly found out when I graduated. That's when you "commence" to have responsibilities, to look for a job, and everything that goes with leaving the nest. And many times this includes the responsibility of a spouse.

Another reason for June weddings may be linked to a primeval urge that's seasonal. As the poet said, "In the spring a young man's fancy lightly turns to thoughts of love." Well, okay. It's true that the delicate scents of spring flowers are linked to the use of perfumes and colognes...To a whole industry, actually.

"Thoughts of love" may be stretching it a bit. It may not be love. We've all known young men whose thoughts in the spring lightly turn to almost anything in tight pants. As the country song says, the girls all look prettier at closing time...Or in the spring.

Another modification of the old adage says that in the spring the young man's fancy "lightly turns" to what the girls have been thinking about all winter. Having raised five daughters, I can attest to this.

You can always tell a person who's in love. Of course, you can't tell them much, and they won't listen anyway. (I really did intend for this column to be a little more serious, but I get carried away.)

Marriage customs in different cultures and times in history vary quite widely. There's a lot of symbolism in some. The couple kindles a fire together. The groom carries the bride over the threshold. In the movie "Roots" the wedding is accomplished when the couple "jumps the broom" which has been placed on the floor. This symbolizes the establishment of a home together.

In recent years in our culture, there is a tendency to modify the traditional church ceremony by adding material written by the couple. I think that's good. If they have to think a little about "what this means to me," it's more meaningful.

I know of several couples who have used material from traditional American Indian ceremonies. These vary widely, because we're looking at more than 300 separate cultures, but some are, quite simply, beautiful. A reader sent me a copy of an "Apache Wedding Ceremony" a while back. She didn't give me a return address, so I can't thank her. This is apparently a closing prayer, used by a Justice of the Peace in Scottsdale, Arizona:

> Now for you there is no rain,
> For one is shelter to the other.
> Now for you there is no darkness,
> For one is counsel to the other.
> Now for you there is no pain,
> For one is comfort to the other.
> Now for you there is no night,
> For one is light to the other.
> Now for you there is no cold,
> For one is warmth to the other.
> Now for you the snow has ended always,
> Your fears, your wants, your needs at rest.
> It is that way...today, tomorrow, forever.
> Now it is good and there is always shelter.
> And now there is always warmth.
> And now there is always comfort.
> Now there is no loneliness.
> Now, forever, forever, you are as one.
>
> There are two bodies but there is one heart
> in both of them and you are the same person.

I thought that this was one of the best of such prayers or blessings that I've seen. It could be used in combination with any religious faith or any civil ceremony, without violating other requirement or tradition. I don't know whether it's really Apache or not. But it says what needs to be said, and says it well. So, does it really matter?

See you down the road.

Road Kill

As I wrote last month, we were in Cheyenne, Wyoming during the famous Frontier Days Rodeo this year. Actually, we didn't even get to see the rodeo, because this was a business trip.

There are thousands of people who converge on Cheyenne for that week, people who might read books about the West. What better way to promote? Five of us writers had decided to try something new, a series of multiple author signing parties in a geographic region like that near Cheyenne, while the crowds were there. We had some pretty big guns…Win Blevins, Earl Murray, Terry C. Johnston, and Richard Wheeler, all names familiar to readers of the West. Terry Johnston had been instrumental in setting up the signings, in Greeley, Longmont, and twice in Cheyenne.

It was in Cheyenne that this lady came by the table where we were all signing books. The final Rodeo parade was going on just outside the book store, City News on Carey Avenue. People were moving in and out, watching the parade awhile and then coming back in to get out of the sun. It was hot that morning.

I first noticed the young woman's T-shirt. It was white with artfully-airbrushed lettering in lavender, black and orange. *"Grand Prize Winner,"* it proclaimed across the chest, along with starbursts of color. *Quadruple Kill!"*

The second time she came past, my curiosity got the best of me. Tell us, I requested, what the inscription means.

The woman was embarrassed, but after all, if you're going to wear something that makes that sort of a statement, you'd better be ready to explain it. She told us the amazing tale.

Several people, friends and family, had driven from Alabama for the Rodeo. She had been driving the van on Interstate 80 in Nebraska. It was twilight, and she saw something moving in the road ahead. A deer, maybe? She started to brake, but was still moving pretty fast when she saw what it was. A family of raccoons was crossing the highway, single file. On her left was an eighteen-wheeler and on her right, a sharp dropoff. There was no chance to swerve, and the van plowed through the column of four 'coons, causing great carnage.

It was really pretty tragic, but it had been a close call. When it was over, the van safely halted and checked for damage, they began to realize that it had been a really dangerous situation for the people. What if the driver had not been able to drive straight ahead, and had clipped the semi or gone over the embankment?

In the process of emotional let-down, the driver began to cry. Naturally her family and friends began to tease her, which probably did help to put the whole thing in perspective. After all, the unfortunate raccoons were not a bad trade-off for six or seven human lives.

They teased her all the way to Cheyenne, marveling at the expertise of a driver so skilled that she could wipe out four raccoons at one stroke.

They finally reached the fairgrounds at Cheyenne and were cruising all the commercial exhibits and booths. Someone spotted a custom T-shirt designer, and they decided to solemnize the trip and the incident. They all chipped in to buy the homicidal driver a specially-designed, commemorative, one-of-a-kind shirt.

It actually was pretty attractive, and will make a nice souvenir. The tale of the narrow escape and the accompanying mayhem among the Nebraska raccoon population will be told and retold for generations as the shirt resurfaces from time to time.

Oh yes, there was an inscription on the back of the shirt, too: *"First Annual Interstate-80 Raccoon Roll."* But, I'll bet they all hope it's also the last one.

See you down the road.

Hair

I need a haircut, and I'll get one one of these days. But, while I was thinking about it, it occurred to me that hair styles, particularly those of men and boys, provide a unique look at our culture, as well as proof of our absolute idiocy.

Traditionally, men have laughed at the devotion of women to what's current in "style." But look at old photographs, high school year-books, historical pictures. The slaves to fashion in hair styles have been the men. A year or two out of date, and a man appears ridiculous.

Our founding fathers are usually depicted in powdered wigs. That was for formal occasions, of course. I don't know what they might have worn around the house on weekends. How would you decide whether to wear your wig or not? What kind of haircut did they wear under it? And Ben Franklin, who apparently *didn't* wear a powdered wig. He was bald on top, and had shoulder length hair around the sides and back. (Now there's an interesting combination.) Powdered wigs were out of style pretty quickly anyway. That was too British for the new nation. Judges, attorneys and lawmakers *still* wear powdered wigs in England, possibly to conceal their identity, I suppose.

Early photographs of frontier figures such as Wild Bill Hickock indicate that many of them wore shoulder-length hair. George Custer is always depicted that way. (I've read that he was *not* scalped at the Little Big Horn fiasco. Some said that it was out of respect and honor, but it was probably because he was bald on top, like Ben Franklin.)

Speaking of scalps, there were a variety of hair styles among American Indians. Several nations shaved the sides and left a roach up the middle, now called "Mohawk." The Indian hand sign for that hair-cut, though, means "Osage." Pawnees shaved the whole head except for a four-inch circle on the top front. This was allowed to grow long, waxed with tallow and paint, and coiled up into a horn-shaped orna-ment. Charles Rivois, a Piegan, reported that a Pawnee was "the easi-est of all to scalp."

Back to our own follies, when I was small, boys' hair was parted in the middle and combed to the sides. A little later, it could be parted on one side or the other, and the larger side combed *back*. Then came World War II, and the military "crew-cut," about an inch long on top and short on the sides. It was comfortable, took little care, and looked pretty good. After the war, it was around for a while, evolving into the "butch" and the flat-top. A spinoff from this was a line of waxes to hold the short hair in an upright stance.

When the Beatles from England came on the scene, they had long shaggy hair and were quite repulsive to most of that generation. It helped them get a lot of attention, though. It's quite remarkable to see how clean-cut and well-groomed they look by today's standards. (Actually, I think there are no "standards.")

Some of the odd aberrations now defy description. The spikes and odd dyeing jobs...Shaving designs and obscenities across the back or one side...One side long, the other shaved...

More discreet but equally idiotic was the onset, a few years back, of a fairly decent haircut, but with one little string in back left long, sticking down over the collar. (Ever want to sneak up and clip off that little wisp?)

Shaving it all off seems to be gaining popularity, especially in sports. Well, that makes sense. You shampoo your hair with a wash cloth. On women who have to do that to get attention, I'm not so sure. There must be a better way. Possibly even talent and hard work.

Well, it's fun to watch. Oh, yes...I heard recently that a porcupine is simply a possum with an attitude and a bad-hair day. Makes sense.

See you down the road.

Somebody Has to Do It   August 1993

After the Western Writers' convention in Springdale, Arkansas this summer, another event was taking shape. It involved another trip, for promotion and publicity.

To back up a little...Two years ago, Bantam Books agreed to sponsor an event at the big Reno Rodeo in Nevada. The rodeo goes on for about ten days, and there's sort of a trade show at the rodeo grounds. Sierra News, a regional distributor of magazines and paperback books, set up a booth there and several of Bantam's authors were rotated through a day at a time, to sign books and visit with the crowd.

This generated a lot of good will and interest. A lot of people stopped by to shake hands and say thanks to Bantam and to Sierra News for their support of the rodeo. Probably this did not result in a lot of immediate book sales. People don't go to a rodeo to buy books. But they do go home, to all parts of the country, and they may buy a book or two as a result of that contact. Considering that upwards of a hundred thousand people attend the Reno Rodeo each year, this could affect nationwide sales considerably. But, it isn't easily identifiable in the statistics. It was decided not to send authors to Reno in 1992.

Sierra News still had their booth, and noticed an interesting fact. A lot of people stopped to inquire about the fact that the writers *weren't* there to talk to folks. So, in 1993 it seemed like a good idea to try it again.

This time there were to be four writers at Reno at the same time. Terry C. Johnston and Earl Murray had already been there for a few days. Win Blevins and I attended the convention in Arkansas and would then fly on to Reno together to join them. (It's a tough job, but somebody has to do it.)

In 1991, Edna had gone with me to Reno. This time it didn't seem practical. We'd have to buy her plane tickets, and connections from Arkansas to Nevada are a bit complicated and expensive. And then, I'd be tied down when we got there, with no chance to run and play. So, she'd take me to the airport at Fayetteville, and then drive home to Emporia.

Anyway, that was the idea. It first began to fall apart when we rose in Springdale the morning of June 25. Our flight was at 9:45 AM out of Fayetteville, and we'd be in Reno early in the afternoon to sign books at the rodeo.

Wrong. There was a major storm front across the map and the airport at Fayetteville was closed. We waited around. Finally we managed to get on a different flight to Dallas, knowing that we'd already missed our connections to Reno. Edna left us at the Fayetteville airport, to start the five-hour trip home to Kansas, after I promised to call her when we got to Reno.

In Dallas, Win Blevins and I managed to get on a plane for Reno. We taxied out to the runway, with a dozen or so planes ahead of us. While our flight was working up toward the runway, the wind began to change. The tail of the storm line that had caused our trouble in Fayetteville now whipped through Dallas. Our plane was second in line to take off when they closed the Dallas airport.

We sat on the plane for the next five hours, waiting for something to happen. They couldn't feed us, because they couldn't bring the carts out into the aisle. They burned so much fuel taxiing around (or standing still) that we had to go back and refuel. It was hot...

We reached Reno about 10 PM, some eight hours late. That's Pacific Time, so we'd had a pretty long day, starting on Central Time. That's what Edna thought too, when I called her about 1 AM, Emporia time.

But they let us sleep in, and the rest of the stay was a wonderful success.

See you down the road.

Western Wedding August 1993

I wrote about a wedding last month, but here's another one. The circumstances were so unique that it deserves a little attention.

At the Western Writers' convention in Jackson, Wyoming in 1992, one of our friends from Michigan met a young woman writer from Missouri. They hit it off pretty well, and kept in touch. In the ensuing year they were able to see each other occasionally, as well as talking via phone and exchanging letters. They began to consider marriage.

Now at this point, you'd have to know the Western Writers of America to understand. This is a family-oriented organization. There are children who have grown up attending the annual convention nearly every year. Some of our lifetime best friends are people whom we've met there. It's an intensive sort of annual get-together which is hard to describe but produces long-lasting effects. So, for our writer friends, it seemed only logical to be married there.

The 1993 convention would be held in Springdale, Arkansas. They began to plan ahead. Why not arrive a day early, ask their guests to do the same, and have the wedding the evening before the first day of the meeting? To make the story short, that's what happened.

Probably fifty people who were to attend the convention arrived through the day of Saturday, June 19, to check in early. Some were agents and editors with whom they have worked. Others, like ourselves, just friends. Then there were a few relatives of the couple, and the wedding party, not all engaged in the publishing business.

They chose for the ceremony a small non-denominational wedding chapel just outside Springdale. It was a nice setting, quiet and intimate, almost crowded, with the number of guests.

There were a few things that were decidedly different about this wedding, though. One was the music, which was taped. It had been chosen by the couple, and prepared by the groom. Since both are engaged in writing about the West, they are oriented to its literature, including print, radio, and movies. The processional was the theme music from the movie *High Noon*..."Do not forsake me, oh my darling, on this our wedding day…"

Music during the ceremony was the haunting flute theme from the Clint Eastwood movie, *The Good, the Bad and the Ugly*. It's a beautiful number. I doubt that the title had any direct connection. (But who knows? Both *had* been married before.)

The bride was given away by the president of Western Writers. I think that was because of his friendship, not because of his office.

The minister did a nice job, considering that this was a pretty unorthodox wedding. It was really a sort of charming event.

We were wondering what sort of music the recessional would be. I thought of several possibilities, but would never have guessed. It was the theme from the old *Lone Ranger* radio show. It brought a ripple of laughter, but somehow, it seemed appropriate.

I guess, in a time when people are being married on roller-coasters, in free-fall parachute jumps, under water, and on horseback, this was pretty mild.

It was a good feeling to think that they were able to accomplish this gathering of friends and associates from all over the country to share their happiness. We all wished them well, on into the evening (and into the night) back at the hotel, in several different celebrations as more friends drifted in.

They seem off to a good start. If this marriage turns out as well as a lot of the others in that group, they should do quite well. Anyway, they'll have a lot of people checking on them annually at the time of their anniversary!

See you down the road.

The Final Exam

We recently received a copy of the introductory issue of a new magazine, *Ad Astra*. Many Kansans will recognize this as the first half of the Kansas motto, *Ad Astra Per Aspera*..."To the Stars Through Difficulties." I'm not writing this column to pass judgment on the new magazine, or to predict the odds on its success or lack thereof. The publishing business is, to say the least, a bizarre occupation, and there's really no way to predict much of anything about the chances of a newborn magazine.

But that's not the purpose of this column. The thing that caught my attention in this premier issue of *Ad Astra* was part of an article on education. It was a "Final exam for Eighth Graders." A real exam, given in Salina, Kansas, in 1895. It's on file in the Smoky Valley Genealogical Society's archives in Salina, says the article.

Arithmetic first caught my eye. I had a few problems with math myself.

1. Name and define the fundamental rules of arithmetic. (What?)
2. A wagon box is 2 ft. deep, 10 ft. long, and 3 ft. wide. How many bushels of wheat will it hold?
3. If a load of wheat weighs 3942 lbs. what is it worth at 50 cts. per bu., deducting 1050 lbs. for tare?

Now I'm sure some readers are thinking that these questions are not appropriate for today's eighth graders. They will never need this sort of knowledge. Okay...

4. District No. 33 has a valuation of $35,000. What is the necessary levy to carry on a school seven months at $50 per month, and have $104 for incidentals?

I couldn't even get past the astonishment of what inflation has done in a century, much less work the problem.

Question 5 involves buying coal, so let's skip to something modern kids will *need* to understand.

6. Find the interest of $512.60 for 8 months and 18 days at 7 percent.

It's likely that most people today would use a computer, calculator, or maybe even a chart. But what if the electricity is off (as in

California…It's coming!) and the battery is weak in the calculator (a common problem); how many homes have such a chart? How many adults would have the faintest idea where to start? (Skip to 9.) What is the cost of a square farm at $15 per acre, the distance around which is 640 rods? (For modern thinking, try $15 *hundred* an acre.)

Some things become apparent here, the first of which is that I would flunk the math part. Let's try Grammar…

1. Give nine rules for the use of Capital Letters. (Might as well forget that one. Nobody uses these rules anymore anyway.)
2. Name the Parts of Speech and define those that have no modifications.
3. Define Verse, Stanza, and Paragraph.
4. What are the Principal Parts of a verb? Give Principal Parts of do, lie, lay and run.
5. Define Case. Illustrate each Case.
6. What is punctuation? Give rules for principal marks of Punctuation.

I think I just flunked English, too. An even longer section is titled "Orthography" and I don't even know what that is.

I do think there's a message here. The American public is rapidly becoming illiterate. I heard a national TV network newscaster say this morning that "…the ship broke in two and *sunk*." I have a file of newspaper clippings with errors such as "the victim was laying in the street…," "he put on the breaks…," "we'll see how his predecessor will handle the job…" (The spellcheck just won't work, folks. It only tells whether it's a *word*, not if it's a *wrong* word.)

And, remember the recent study which showed that the average American 14-year-old knows the meaning of fewer than half as many words as kids the same age a generation ago?

What's the answer? I don't know. I'm sure that the problem can't be stated in simple terms either. I have an idea that it's part of the entire current approach to responsibility, often demonstrated by public figures: "It wasn't my fault, it was somebody else…A conspiracy…The *teacher's* fault." Our legal system encourages this. How about we give the teachers back the authority to discipline and to teach, and *let them teach*. It would be a start.

See you down the road.

Things
of the Spirit

The Day The World Changed   October 2001

Usually, about the middle of each month, I mail out next month's Horsin' Around columns to the subscribing newspapers. We were just about ready to do so with the columns for October, 2001. I turned on the TV for the morning news and saw a live picture of the twin towers of the World Trade Center. One was smoking, and there were unverified rumors that it had been struck by an aircraft of some sort. From there, the day began to fall apart, and the world would never be the same again.

We watched the second plane on live television as it hit the second towering building. At that point, we had been preparing to board a plane to Chicago in a few hours for a lecture and book signing. All our thoughts of climbing on a plane to anywhere quickly dissolved, even before air traffic was officially grounded.

People were already beginning to compare this to the bombing of Pearl Harbor, which had been my first reaction. I also realized that I needed, for my own peace of mind, to *write* about it, before mailing October's columns. By the time you read this, there will have been many other events, I'm sure.

There are major events that mark the course of our lives. Everyone who was old enough to remember when the President was assassinated can tell you exactly where he/she was when the news came. In my lifetime, probably the three biggest events so far have been 1) Pearl Harbor 2) The atom bomb, and 3) Man's landing on the moon. Of these, probably the atom bomb was most important.

I was a teenager, a combat medic in a Tank Destroyer battalion in the Philippines. The fighting had calmed down, things were pretty secure, and the medical detachment was holding morning "sick call" for the usual aches, pains, minor injuries, and ever-present skin rashes in the tropical climate. We were listening to Armed Forces Radio, which had pretty good programming. Music, news, occasionally "Tokyo Rose," the seductive female voice of the Japanese propaganda network, telling us that our wives and girlfriends were sleeping with draft dodgers back home, and that we'd all be killed soon unless we surrendered. These broadcasts were certainly effective, in two different ways. They were good for our morale in opposite directions. They were funny. Tokyo Rose, for instance, in telling us how low the morale was on the home front, would manufacture bad news: People in the area of Coffeyville, Kansas, she once told us, were starving because of the failure of the season's coffee crop. I had to explain the joke to a few of the Californians.

The other extreme was that of anger. Some of the guys, naturally worried about wives and families, became fighting mad at the suggestion they surrender. We already knew what had happened to troops who surrendered to Japanese. But, we were ready to invade.

The radio interrupted some pretty good music to report that an entirely new kind of bomb, an "atomic fission" device, had been dropped on the city of Hiroshima. Some of the men scoffed at this report as some of our own propaganda. But our old battalion surgeon, who had been "through the islands," made an observation that I've recalled many times.

"Boys," he said, "mark this day, because the world will never be the same again."

It took only a short while to realize that now, maybe we'd live to go home. We wouldn't have to invade Japan. With all of the destruction and carnage caused by the atom bombs, millions more lives, both Americans and Japanese, were *saved* than destroyed. Mine was one of those, so to me there can never be an ethical doubt about the president's decision to drop the bomb.

We've watched a tragedy unfold in recent days. We'll have tougher times ahead, but it has been encouraging to see a sudden rise of patriotism. Recruitment offices with waiting lines...*Flags*...People helping each other...Crowds in churches, synagogues, *and mosques*... Even unheard-of joint services, as legitimate Muslim worshipers of the same God join the Judeo-Christian congregations. Let us be sure to realize that the "Muslim" perpetrators of this horror are no more legitimate Muslims than some of the lunatic cults who sometimes call themselves Christian are really Christian.

And the crops still grow at Coffeyville.

See you down the road.

Blassus Fudd

As a preacher's kid I learned about table grace very early. At every meal the family gathered at the table, as most families did then, and bowed our heads in a prayer of thanks for food. Even the youngest child participated in this ritual. As soon as a child could begin to talk, it started with a simple "Thank you for the food. Amen," alone or in unison.

Now I was third in sequence in a family of four kids. As early as I can remember we used a unison prayer, "Bless this food, keep us today. Amen." My older siblings sort of rushed it along, so that it came out something like "Blassus-fudd-key-buster-day-amen."

The "amen" marked it as a ritual of some importance. It must be because we said that in church, too. But the rest was a jumble of sounds whose meaning was a complete puzzle. I can recall trying to reason out those ritual words to the Blassus Fudd ceremony.

I could figure out parts of it, like the Amen, but the rest gave me real problems. Who was Buster Day, for example? There was a short while when I had him confused with Buster Brown, whose picture appeared in shoe advertisements with his dog, Tige. There was also Buster Keaton in the movies, although we didn't often see a movie. I decided that there must be several people named Buster. Some day I might learn what this one had to do with a table ritual and food.

The "key" part was easier. I knew about keys. A key was the shiny brass thing that jingled in my dad's pocket. He'd put it in the dashboard of our old Dodge car with the wooden wheels. When he turned it, the engine started. Obviously, an object of great power, very fitting in a prayer ritual. Maybe it was used to somehow implore the efforts of Buster Day in our behalf.

Blassus Fudd remained a complete mystery. I think I must have classed it along with other ceremonial words used in churchly situations, which had no apparent translations of their own. Like hymn or anthem or hallelujah…a table grace became, in my childish mind, a Blassus Fudd.

I'm sure some readers are wondering whether there's a point to all this marginal blasphemy. Of course there is. The point is that it *worked*. It drove home to me the importance of thanks for food.

In our own home, our children grew up saying a table grace, usually in unison. I'm sure some of them use a thanks for food in their homes, with their children. Edna and I still say grace over every meal.

Sure, people seldom eat meals formally at a family table now. Often families gather in front of the TV for a hurried snack before dispersal to all the meetings and activities which have replaced family evenings at home. We often eat while we watch the evening news. But we can turn it off for a moment to say the brief ritual prayer, and we do.

I think most families have a tendency to do so more often when it's a special meal of some sort. Like a birthday or an anniversary or a holiday meal such as Christmas or Thanksgiving dinner. On such occasions it seems only appropriate to give thanks for our bounty. That, of course, is what Thanksgiving is all about. To give thanks for all that we have, especially food. We are better off in that respect than any country in the world, probably...Quality, availability, cost...

There's something about Thanksgiving that is special. Probably the harvest festival goes back to prehistoric times. It includes the thanks to God for successful crops and a successful hunt, and a hope for survival through another winter.

A special meal involves a special spiritual feeling in us, if we can slow down from the hectic pace long enough to allow it. It invokes a need to recognize this feeling.

Maybe that's why, when I see and smell the wonderful sights and scents of Thanksgiving, it takes me back to the special meals of my childhood. The phrase of prayerful thanks flits through my mind and I murmur in worshipful gratitude, "Blassus Fudd."

See you down the road.

Downright Unchristian

For several weeks not long ago, I followed with interest a situation reported via Letters to the Editor, in a small town weekly newspaper. I'll not identify the paper or the community involved, because it doesn't matter anyway, and it's far from here.

The first letter I saw was in response to a hate letter which had been sent to the Chief of the volunteers of their Fire Protection District. The exact text of the hate letter was never disclosed, but it was apparently an attempt to cause trouble among the personnel of the volunteer fire department. Like most of those who stoop to such activities, this perpetrator had not signed the poison-pen epistle. (In fact, poison pens having become obsolete by the advance of technology, this one was composed on a computer. The computer lends itself well to such anonymity, chicanery, and cowardice.) The letter was mailed from a large city some distance from the community involved, further delineating the character of the perpetrator.

The letter itself was not printed in the paper, but apparently implied or even threatened that there was trouble in the Fire District. A copy was sent to each member of the Fire District board. It threatened that if certain of the volunteer firemen were not removed immediately, there would be a wholesale resignation by a dozen or more of the other firemen. Why the objection by the hate-monger? The person or persons that he (she?) wanted to remove were of *another religion*. How stupid can even a writer of hate mail get? I'll state right now that if my house was on fire, and a truck with firemen arrived, I would not stop them to determine that I approve of their church affiliation, sexual proclivities, politics, or anything else. Let 'em put out the fire! I wouldn't care if they're Jewish or Buddhists or Muslim or Shinto or even atheists, if they're ready and willing to extinguish the blaze.

But this self-appointed trouble-maker wanted to banish the fireman, because he's not a Christian, but a Mormon...Wait a minute! Who is a Christian, here, anyway? One would think that a person whose beliefs include the Holy Trinity of Father, Son and Holy Spirit, salvation through Christ, and Baptism are very likely Christians. Not so, according to some. I'm a lifelong Methodist, except for when I once preached in a Congregational church for a year, but I have been told that I'm not a Christian. Christians have some problems with defining themselves. Not all Christians, of course. Some are quite tolerant. But some insist that anyone who doesn't believe exactly as they do can't claim to be Christian at all. I've always felt that I'm not entirely qualified to evaluate what God said to somebody else, only what He said to me. (Who was it that said "Judge not, lest you be judged?")

I'll probably be in trouble for this column. It's not smart to discuss one's religion or politics. Maybe this is both.

So, what happened to the Fire Protection District with the hate mail? It was some time before the Chief wrote a letter to the newspaper to clarify the situation. He told about the letter, and how there had been no resignations. There had been an outpouring of support from the community, both for the firemen and for the Latter Day Saints Church, the "Mormons." A few letters from Mormons, whose specialty is helping not only each other, but anyone in trouble.

One woman, (not a Mormon), wrote in detail about the wonderful Christmas celebration, participated in by all the churches in the area, a joint service at the Church of Latter Day Saints. This is a sparsely settled region, and people are important to each other, regardless of differences. It's hard to cause division in that sort of community, because they need each other.

Maybe it's significant that there was not one letter in support of the hate-monger. I'm not sure what the writer of that letter hoped to accomplish. Maybe he lives there, maybe not. But regardless, I'll bet he knows a lot more about that community than he did. Regardless of religion, these are folks who'll look after their own...*All* of their own.

See you down the road.

Strong Medicine October 2001

It has long been a custom, in many different cultures and religions, to pray for those who are sick or afflicted. This comes in many forms, even to extremes of "faith healing." With all the emphasis, during the last century or so, on the importance of the sciences, such evidence of faith often fell by the wayside. If you couldn't weigh or measure or graph the results, it was presumed that they didn't exist. Something that isn't tangible enough to be held, felt, seen or smelled simply isn't there, to many people. There's a tendency to suggest that somehow science and religion are incompatible. If one is valid, the other can't be. This leads to ridiculous arguments about "evolution" and "creation," which are in essence the same thing, told from two valid yet different points of view.

This must have been very confusing to the American Indian cultures, and possibly quite amusing. There are more than 300 such cultures, but all are similar in some respects. They are quite aware of the spiritual presence of a Supreme Being. This is closely related to healing, and to well-being in general. Spiritual power is included in the Indian expression "medicine,." There is no word in English that can express everything that is implied in "medicine." (English is in many ways quite limited when compared to some of the languages used by American Indians.) A "medicine man" (or woman) has not only a knowledge and skill in healing, but is a priest, counselor, advisor, teacher, and prophet, in tune with what Christians would call the Holy Spirit. To them, it's all the same continuum.

By contrast, European cultures tried so hard to become pragmatic over the sciences that they began to neglect the obvious influence of spiritual power. For a while, this was especially true in medicine. There were physicians, as well as patients, of course, who felt otherwise. They were pretty quiet about it, to avoid ridicule.

In the past few decades, however, there has been a lot of recognition on the part of "scientific" medicine that it had become too limited. Modern hospitals on Indian reservations invited Indian doctors as consultants. This led to some discoveries. For example, that the mysterious new "hanta" virus had been known to the Indian medicine men for centuries, (including the fact that it is carried by mice, only discovered by Science in the past decade or two.)

Of course, prayer and ritual are a part of any American Indian healing ceremony. In the past few years, several studies have been carried out under scientific control which evaluated and systematically demonstrated the efficacy of prayer. In thousands of cases, comparison studies showed mathematical results that were astounding. A new medicine which would produce similar improvements in recovery statistics would be hailed as a miracle drug.

An important factor to me was that there was no correlation between the pray-er and pray-ee. It was tried both ways...Catholics praying for Catholics, Baptists for Baptists, Muslims for Muslims, etc. But, also, as a control for the experiments, random assignment. Somehow, it turned out that it was equally effective. Christians praying for Buddhists, Jews for Muslims...It did not seem to make any statistical difference at all. Only that a prayer was offered for the patient, whatever his faith. (That is really going to be a threat to some, I'm sure.)

Recently, a relative of friends here was diagnosed with a far advanced colon cancer. She was treated with chemotherapy and x-ray, but given a very gloomy prognosis. Major surgery, colostomy, terribly poor chances, terrible news for an attractive woman in her forties. But her family and friends, via e-mail, snail mail, phone and fax, all available means of communication, established a prayer chain. I'm sure it included those of many different beliefs. But all agreed to "turn up the volume" of prayer at a certain time: The morning that "Jane" would be wheeled into surgery in Texas to begin the exploratory operation. On the gurney cart, covered by a blue blanket, on the way to the OR, she sleepily whispered to her husband: *They won't find anything!*"

They didn't. Not even anything to biopsy. She'll be followed closely, of course, but the prognosis has certainly improved. Powerful "medicine."

See you down the road.

The Evolution of Santa

Our Judeo-Christian culture has a strange way of absorbing and modifying bits of other cultures and religions until they become completely unrecognizable. Santa Claus, for example, is probably the most recognizable symbol of crass commercialism that exists. Yet he was a real person, a Christian Saint, who has been through a remarkable sequence of change. Somehow, Christmas has taken on a sort of Old English flavor for us, with holly and mistletoe and Charles Dickens and carolers. And Santa, of course. Most people don't realize that Saint Nicholas was actually *Turkish*...The Bishop of Myra, a small town in Lycia, about 300 A.D. He apparently ascended to the bishop's office while very young, and is known as the "boy bishop." He became the patron saint of schoolboys, and then of all children. In Germany, he became *Pelz Nichol*, translated "Nicholas in fur," and described as a hairy elf. Parents tell Pelz Nichol how their children behave, and receive presents or switches as they deserve. The Santa Claus name is a corruption of *Sinter Klaas*, which is Dutch for Saint Nicholas. Santa's appearance and mode of transport have changed considerably. Originally a tall, slender and stately figure in bishop's robes, he rode a white donkey. Dutch settlers in New York had a somewhat different idea, developed by the writer Washington Irving. Irving, who described Saint Nicholas as the "guardian of New York" saw him as a plump jolly man who looked much like a Dutch settler... Broad-brimmed hat, baggy breeches, smoking a pipe...This *Sinter Klaas* drove a wagon and a team of horses *across the sky* and dropped presents down chimneys. In 1822, Clement C. Moore wrote the poem "A Visit From St. Nicholas" for his own children. We know it as "The night before Christmas." Now if you actually *read* it, Santa doesn't have a red suit. He's "dressed all in fur," like Pelz Nichol, and is described as an elf. He has traded his horse team for an eight-hitch of miniature reindeer, and his wagon for a sleigh. Paintings a few years later begin to show him in knee boots and with fur *trim* on his suit, which is often green or red. An old jumping jack toy, made by my grandfather, shows a more slender Santa with a red coat, *blue* trousers, and boots which are laced to the knees. The fur trim on his coat is ermine, like that on a king's robes. This Santa doesn't look very jolly, probably because of job pressures. Saint Nicholas was actually deported from England by King Henry VIII when the king withdrew from the Roman Catholic church to found the Church of England. Celebrations of the feast day of Saint Nicholas, December 6, became illegal. Somewhat later, Queen Victoria reincarnated him, but as "Father Christmas," a British-looking gentleman in a long-tailed coat and square-topped beaver hat. In another strange twist, the Protestant Reformation in Europe replaced the Saint with the Christ-child, *Christkindle* in German. This figure became *Kris Kringle*, who in some parts of Europe brings gifts and is sometimes *accompanied* by a hairy elf, Pelz Nichol!

By this time it's getting hard to tell what it's all about. We have the original Saint, as well as Kris Kringle, Pelz Nichol, Sinter Klaas, Santa and Father Christmas. Some of these may be the same individual (or not). Sometimes they accompany each other. To further complicate the scene, other English-speaking countries, (i.e. England, Canada, and Australia) have popularized the American version of Santa Claus. They may have both Santa and Father Christmas. One last bit of Christmas trivia: Early in this century, United States banks could (and did) print their own currency. It was accepted as legal tender. In New York City was the Bank of Saint Nicholas, named for the Saint whom Washington Irving depicted as the "Guardian of New York City."At one time the Bank of Saint Nicholas printed a three-dollar bill. They chose for the portrait on it, their patron saint. This is not likely to come up in ordinary conversation. But, if anyone ever happens to ask you who has his picture on a three dollar bill, you'll know: It's Santa Claus!

Merry Christmas

Things of the Spirit   July 1994

A while back I was contacted as a potential speaker by a friend who lived in Emporia a few years ago. It seems that he had been talking to one of the members of their church in the Kansas City area and discovered a mutual connection. The other church member is related to us by marriage.

We hadn't seen either of them for many years. We eventually managed to work out a date a few months ahead. It was, however, my first experience in speaking to a Unitarian church. That didn't really bother me. I've spoken through the years to all different sorts of audiences: Teachers of English, Social Studies, and History...a genealogical society...the Kansas Fish Growers and the Kansas Herpetological Society...the Kansas Flying Farmers...Well, you get the idea.

When I get a little apprehensive about speaking to a group I know nothing about, I always fall back on a remark by my wife some years ago. We were traveling to another town where I was to speak at a church. I mentioned that I wasn't sure what they'd expect. A lecture, or a sermon? Edna suggested not to worry about it. If they wanted a real preacher, she said, they'd have asked one. Well, okay...

I was faced with that sort of thing on this occasion, but I did have a topic. They had asked me to talk about American Indian religions, so I had a general direction.

I could write an entire column about their facility in Shawnee Mission, beautiful grounds and buildings. Their offices are in a stately old stone farmhouse and the church is the remodeled stone barn adjacent to it. They were on a summer schedule, with no minister or choir. (I don't know whether they have a choir or not, normally.) The prelude was a very impressive taped concert number on the PA system. While it played, I was glancing through their hymnal. It occurred to me that I couldn't find any hymns which mentioned Christ, and that there were no crosses anywhere.

I whispered this to the former Emporian beside me. "Oh, no," he explained, "we're not Christian." Just then he stood up to introduce me.

I don't startle very easily, but I was surprised. I somehow had the idea that Unitarians were a Christian splinter group. There was no problem, really, because I was to talk about things not related to their religion or mine, anyway. But it did stir my curiosity.

A bit of research later revealed that I was pretty close in my impression. The Unitarian Universalist Association was formed in 1961, by the merger of the two groups. Both have their roots in early Christian writings. The Unitarians rose from the liberal wing of the Congregational Churches of New England, merging with some Episcopal groups in the late 1700s. Their principle point of contention was to reject the idea of the Trinity, (as some early Christian writers did. God is one, not three, they insisted.)

Universalism, an offshoot of the Church of England, is based on the hypothesis that everyone will eventually experience what fundamentalist Christians call "salvation." They reject the idea of atonement for sin. Not surprisingly, Ralph Waldo Emerson and his Transcendentalist movement of the last century was closely associated with this group.

After the merger, these two organizations became one, with some basic philosophies: God is one…Unity. Jesus is recognized, but as human, not a deity. There is a basic belief in man's ability to overcome error by reason. (This makes the group appealing to many intellectuals, though I doubt that everyone has the reasoning capacity to handle it.)

Most importantly, their principle that individuals should be free to form their own religious beliefs. I'll get some criticism on this one, but I think it's true. I shouldn't be able to tell you what you believe, any more than I'd allow you to tell me what I believe. God speaks to different people in different ways. That's what the American Indian religions are about, but it also reminds me of a Hindu saying:"There are many paths to the top of the mountain, but they all lead to the top of the mountain."

See you down the road.

Hot Times

We had a hot time at our church not long ago. We had just had a church business meeting to discuss some proposed improvements and deferred maintenance problems that were in need of attention. A major concern was the failing heating and air conditioning system.

The following Sunday, with late summer heat near three digits, it was found that the air conditioning had given up the ghost. (No disrespect to the Trinity intended.) There was some discussion as to whether the preacher had shut it down to prove a point, or maybe he'd just asked God to do so. Or possibly, just divine intervention without request.

In any case, it was hot in the sanctuary. It was recalled that a generation ago, nobody had air conditioning anyway. Cooling, in churches, was accomplished with cardboard fans on a stick. These were supplied by the local funeral homes, and carried pictures of Jesus, Noah, Moses, or the Virgin Mary; the latter especially in Catholic or Episcopal settings. This helped to stir the air, and nobody knew any better anyway. (Much like the Depression. Everybody was poor, but nobody knew it, because they were all in the same situation.)

All the talk of cardboard fans and hot church services caused me to recall a situation which involved one of my brothers. This was my preaching brother, not the one who was a writer and journalist. (You may insert at this point any appropriate comment about siblings who took separate paths to the extremes, about evil twins, or whatever. They weren't twins, and I take no responsibility for the actions of either one.)

This event took place in a church in a small town in north central Kansas, which shall remain unnamed. It was just after the end of World War II, before air conditioning became commonplace. This particular church had more of a problem than average, because of an odd architectural design. The platform and the pulpit, at the front of the sanctuary, are directly in front of the choir loft. The choir, the minister, and anybody else on the platform are tucked away, mostly in a sort of alcove, with poor circulation of air. No windows there, so no way at all to circulate air on a hot Sunday morning. Even the congregation in the pews had a better shot at it than the preacher and the choir.

My brother was resourceful. He acquired an electric fan, the oscillating kind that would swing back and forth, and placed it on the edge of the platform, facing the congregation. They still used the fans from the funeral home, but it was a great step in modernization to have the big electric fan sweeping across the sanctuary.

Now, I have to pause to reveal a couple of things about my preaching brother. He had a lot of other interests. He would probably have made a good engineer or scientist. He was skilled as a machinist, auto mechanic, gunsmith, on and on...

What the congregation did not know was that he had reversed the polarity on the oscillating fan. The air from the whirling blades was blowing, not across the congregation, but backward, to benefit the preacher and the long-suffering choir in the stuffy alcove.

A few years ago, I was asked to speak at that same church, at a centennial celebration or something. The architecture hadn't changed, though they did have air conditioning now. I recalled the story of the fan, and shared it with the congregation. Many of them remembered my brother, and recalled that he had a fan on the platform. One man came up afterward, who had been in that choir. The choir, he assured me, knew about the fan's improved design, and the mild deception of the congregation. "But we weren't talkin' about it."

See you down the road.

The Interim Preacher October 1993

I was asked recently to say a few words at the anniversary celebrations of two different churches, one week apart. One was their centennial, the other their 125th. One was Methodist, one Congregational. One is in Tonganoxie, the other in Lancaster.

Actually these churches seem to have very little connection, except that both are in Kansas. There's one other thing, though, I had served as a minister for both. That's a bit unusual, too, because I'm not a clergyman, never wanted to be, and never intended to be. In my own defense, I'll state up front that both of these churches were made aware of that fact. They knew it was a duck egg when they hatched it, so to speak. They had only themselves to blame.

But back to the beginning. I came home from the army after World War II, and enrolled in college at Baker University, in Baldwin, Kansas. During the summer before my senior year in 1948, my dad approached me with a proposition. At the time he was a District Superintendent of the Methodist Episcopal church, in northeast Kansas. They were shorthanded that year, he told me, and he had a few churches that were without ministers. Specifically, would I help him by filling the pulpits on one of his three-church circuits, Effingham-Lancaster-Broyles? Just Sundays, two of the three each week, on a rotating schedule. Just for ten months, until the next Annual Conference, when he hoped to have more real preachers. I'd be paid ten dollars, and somebody would take me home to Sunday dinner each week.

That sounded pretty good. I had just bought my first car, a 1936 Chevy, and needed gas and tires. I'd been on stage quite a bit with a vocal quartet (we'd nearly gone professional with that), and had done some public speaking. I was preparing to go into a professional YMCA job.

It did work out pretty well. Some magnificent Sunday dinners, too. I went to work for the YMCA in Topeka, the following year.

About five years later, I was in the process of changing vocations and was going back to school, attending classes at KU for a year. I had a wife and small daughter by that time, so I was looking for 1) a place to live and 2) a part-time job.

Somehow I heard that the Congregational church in Tonganoxie, a few miles northeast of Lawrence, was in need of a minister. Moreover, they had a pretty good parsonage. I decided to check it out.

I preached for them a couple of times, went over to talk to the state office of their denomination in Topeka, and we worked out a deal. I was actually given authority to perform the sacraments, (they needed a preacher pretty badly) and would receive a small salary and the parsonage to live in. They hadn't had a full time minister for some twenty years, and no one in residence for at least a few.

That worked out pretty well too. I already had a mail order gunsmithing business part-time, and continued that. That next spring and summer I worked part-time at the bait shop and boat rental at the state lake. One way or another, I convinced them that they needed to raise the budget and recruit a real preacher.

There was one interesting event shortly after we moved into the church parsonage, though. A friend with whom I'd worked for several summers was living at Leavenworth, nearby. We'd sort of lost contact for a few years.

Paul had heard by the grapevine that I was in Tonganoxie, but not *what* I was doing there. He placed a person-to-person phone call, via live operators then, of course. The operator rang the Congregational minister's home and asked for me by name. I admitted who I was, and the next sound was Paul's voice:

"What the hell are you doing in Tonganoxie?"

The sound after that was a startled gasp from the operator. With that kind of a start in a town the size of Tonganoxie, I wondered if they'd let me stay. But as I said, they needed a preacher pretty badly.

See you down the road. **DC** ⌣

Fully Loaded

As I write this, the hunting season is in progress. Deer are every-where, and the skilled management of the harvest by the Wildlife and Parks biologists will (hopefully) result in a reduction of the overpop-ulation. These people, biologists and hunters, do a great job, which is not really recognized or appreciated by a great many uninformed but self-appointed "environmentalists," assorted animal rights fanatics, and vegetarians.

A generation ago, nearly every household had at least one hunter. There were more guns by far in proportion to population than there are now, but far less trouble, with far fewer restrictive laws. There was a sense of responsibility for one's own actions which is lacking today. Hunting also put some groceries on most tables.

I recently recalled an adventure that I became involved in while I was in college. I had come home from the Army, and was attending Baker University, on the G.I. Bill. I'd had some experience in gun-smithing, both military and civilian, and was doing quite a bit of gun repair and maintenance for friends and local hunters, for moderate fees.

During my senior year, I had bought a venerable 1936 Chevrolet for $125, which provided me some transportation. My parents lived in Kansas City, Kansas, where my dad was a District Superintendent in the Methodist church. That year, I'd drive up to see them occasional-ly, and he approached me with an offer. He had an acute shortage of young preachers to fill some of the part-time positions in the area. Would I be interested in doing a bit of public speaking? No strings attached...They'd know I wasn't a real preacher, but it would pay ten dollars a week, enough to pay for gas and tires. Three churches... Effingham, Lancaster, and Broyles...Rotating, two of the three each Sunday. I'd be invited to Sunday dinner somewhere. It worked out pretty well, and I learned a lot that year.

At Christmas, I was going home for the holidays, and I had sever-al rifles and shotguns that needed minor work. I decided to take them with me to the folks' place, along with my tool kit, and do the repairs. I laid the guns out on a blanket in the back seat, and covered them with another blanket. My dad had called to tell me that my sister, who was in graduate school in Illinois, was coming in on the train to the Union Station, and I offered to pick her up en route home. I had one thing to do on the way out of Baldwin. I had worked on an antique revolver for somebody. I paused to test fire it, and stuck it in the glove compartment of the Chevy as I started on down the road.

I hit downtown Kansas City, Missouri, just after dark on a chilly December eve. Unfamiliar with the area, I ran a stop light, and was quickly aware of lights and sirens. I pulled over, and two officers approached, one on each side of my car. While one questioned me about a license, the other was shining a flashlight in through the windows on the passenger side. Suddenly he yelled, yanked the door open and ordered me out of the car. Just under my nose was the muzzle of a very large revolver. It seems that the blanket had slid off the cargo in my back seat.

They didn't actually cuff me, but had me assume the search position with hands on the car. While they patted me down for concealed weapons, I tried to explain that I was an innocent college student trying to make ends meet by doing gun repair. They really went into orbit when they found the revolver, still loaded, in my glove compartment. They wanted to know what other source of income I had, and didn't seem to accept the idea that I was a part-time preacher very readily. They stuffed me in the patrol car, asking for some proof of my "connection with the church." I had nothing, beyond some sermon notes for next Sunday, in my suitcase. About that time their radio began to sound off, pretty frantically…A bigger problem than a gun-toting student preacher, I guess. They pushed me out, and took off in a blaze of sirens and flashing lights. They didn't even take time to give me a ticket for running the stop light.

I picked up my sister on time at the Union Station. You win some…
See you down the road.

Leslie

I'm frequently asked at lectures or on book signing occasions, which of my three dozen books is my own favorite. It's a great deal like "Which is your favorite of your children?" If you had one, you couldn't or shouldn't say. But the question isn't logical. We relate to others in a variety of ways. We can enjoy one friend for a sense of humor, another for an appreciation of food, art, music, sports, or for gifts and talents…a singing voice, skills in art or drama or cooking or parenting. As I think of our five daughters, there are a lot of differences. Some are physical. For years, I've written in their birthday cards and on similar occasions, things such as "To my favorite blue-eyed daughter"…or red-headed or green-eyed or curly-haired, etc. There's only one of each. There are three with brown eyes, but this is offset by curly hair or other characteristics. It comes out even.

It's not quite as easy when we come to describe individuals by qualities that have value in themselves. If we're talking about courage or sensitivity or compassion and assign it to one, it implies that the others *don't* have it, which is untrue. It's sure to hurt somebody's feelings, or to imply favoritism. I rarely write about our girls (or our grandchildren), except as part of another story. This time, I'll make an exception. All of this to introduce the fact that I'm writing about one of our daughters, for whom I have an immense amount of respect and admiration. I don't want to downgrade any of the others, but to call attention to some special qualities in this one.

This particular girl came along at a very difficult time, with major upheaval in the family which lasted several years. I was finishing my schooling, and trying to establish a professional practice in Emporia. It all contributed to a quite unusual and traumatic early childhood for this one. In gaming terms, she'd been dealt a poor hand. I long ago decided, though, that in the complicated game of life, we score points on how we play the hand we're dealt. If the world hands you a lemon, make lemonade, Ann Landers once said. In this case, the girl reacted unpredictably, and was estranged from the family for a while. She rejoined as a mature young woman with a husband. They've been a good team, working together to build their own corporation, which now employs some 200 people. They have made us proud, and have also presented us with an obviously superior grandson.

A few years ago she was diagnosed with a breast cancer. She took it in stride, even the hair loss from chemotherapy. She scorned the idea of a wig, preferring to show the world she could handle anything. (Her hair grew back curlier, much to her delight.) We have been impressed with the efficacy of prayer in such situations. This girl's prayer chain seemed to reach around the world. She's appreciated by everyone, of nearly every faith. I mentioned to a woman with whom I work in the publishing industry that there were Methodists and Baptists and Catholics, even a Buddhist friend or two. The instant response: "Well, add a New York Jew!"

The recurrence came a year or so later. More therapy, cell transplants, new experimental treatments, another after another. I could not fail to note that of all our family, not one would be able to handle all of this so well. Her emotional strength, courage, and sense of humor have been an inspiration to us all. She has already beaten the statistical odds, and is going strong. When her oncologist finally told her there was really nothing more to try, her reaction was typical. She called to tell us, and went on to say that she'd let us know when she was going to inform a couple of her sisters...One in particular, "Because *she'll* need you."

She now has some good days and ones not so good, but an occasional pleasant surprise...No transfusion needed this week, and she and her husband are to take off on a second honeymoon to Las Vegas, as I write this.

One of the women in the prayer chain commented on this: "Miracles happen. *I'm* not ready to quit." Neither is the patient, but she's now ready for whatever happens, and she's tired. She recommended a book, *The Next Place*, which is built around a poem by Warren Hanson. "It will make you feel better," she said.

Do you realize, I asked Edna...She is actually organizing a support group for *us?* Now *there's* a special person.

See you down the road.

Good Times and Goodbyes

January 2001

There's a thread of philosophy in some of the oriental religions that suggests that nothing is ever all good or all bad, compared to other things. This is illustrated by an ancient Chinese story:

A man told his neighbor that his stallion had escaped and run away. "That's too bad."

"No, that's good. The stallion returned with three fine wild mares."

"That's good!"

"No, my son tried to ride one of the mares, and suffered a broken leg."

"Too bad…"

"No, that's good. The next day the soldiers came to conscript him for the army. He could not go to war because of the leg."

This story could go on and on. There have been times in my life that looked pretty bleak, but later actually turned out well.

A few weeks ago I wrote a column about our daughter Leslie, who was fighting a recurrent breast cancer. It was a difficult thing to write, but Edna urged me to write it then so that Leslie could appreciate my admiration for her. I thought of William Allen White, writing his classic essay about the death of his daughter Mary, and how hard that must have been.

It was only about an hour after the *Emporia Gazette* was distributed with my column about Leslie, that the phone began to ring. People were relating to our situation. It made me more certain of what I'd suspected, that readers of a columnist's work sometimes become almost like family. We began to receive calls and cards and letters from people who read the column in other papers in Kansas and Missouri. Then, even from other states, from relatives and friends of people who had clipped the column and sent it on. Weeks later, there was still an occasional note…More response than from almost anything I ever wrote. A lot of "thank you for understanding and for saying how we, too, felt at such a time."

In early December we found a few rare days with nothing on our schedule, and decided to make a quick trip to Denver to see how Leslie was doing. We called ahead for hotel reservations and headed west.

Her attitude was still great, though she was frustrated with her increasing disability. It's tougher on someone who has been a go-getter. She was having more pain, too. Despite all this, she rallied to the point of going out to dinner…A Cajun restaurant that she'd been wanting to show us. (She and her husband have *never* steered us wrong on food.) We had a wonderful evening, and a visit we all enjoyed. We spent another day there, enjoying the visit with our six-year-old grandson, and headed on home.

Less than 48 hours later we were wakened early. Intuition told me…Leslie had, as our Indian friends might say, "crossed over." Though it was no surprise, we're never really prepared. At least, we told each other, our visit was well timed. That was the good part. We'd enjoyed the time together, said goodbye, and now she doesn't have to hurt anymore.

For some reason, I thought of a little five-year-old girl we know, who lost an older friend last year, almost an extra grandma. The child's mother explained that Evelyn had died and that they wouldn't be seeing her anymore, that she was now in heaven.

"With Jesus?"

"Yes."

The child was very quiet for a long time, sitting and rocking her doll. Then she approached her mother.

"Can we say a prayer for Evelyn?"

"Would you like to say one?"

There was a short pause.

"Okay…Jesus, we have a friend, Evelyn, who died and is up there with you. We're sad because we won't see her any more. But, if you could take good care of her we'd all feel better and we'd be happy again. Thank you! Amen."

Could it be said any better?
See you down the road.

Don Coldsmith

Don Coldsmith has written some forty books, 150 magazine articles, and 1600 newspaper columns over the last thirty-one years. There are now more than six million copies in print, as well as British, German, and French editions of his historical Western novels, mostly with American Indian themes.

photo by *Homestead Magazine*, published by John Deere, Inc.

Born in Iola, Kansas, to a Methodist minister's family, Coldsmith graduated from High School at Coffeyville, and entered the Army in 1944. He served as a combat medic in the Pacific in World War II, and was among the first troops to enter Japan after the war's end. He was assigned the primary medical care of about forty upper echelon war crimes prisoners, including Premier Hideki Tojo.

Returning to school, he graduated from Baker University in 1949. Working as a YMCA youth director, he initiated the first interracial swimming in Topeka, Kansas, in the same school district as the now-famous "Brown Case," but somewhat earlier.

After a taste of several other vocations he returned to school again, earning a doctorate in medicine in 1958. He served as a physician in Family Practice in Emporia, Kansas, closing his office in 1988 to devote more time to his writing.

Coldsmith is a Past President of Western Writers of America, and has taught in the Division of English, Emporia State University. He has been a finalist six times for the Western Writers' Golden Spur award, and won the Spur for best original paperback of 1990, *The Changing Wind*. He was chosen Distinguished Kansan of 1993 by the Native Sons and Daughters of Kansas, received the Edgar Wolfe Award for lifetime contribution to literature in 1995, and was inducted into the Writers Hall of Fame of America in 2000. He was listed among the twenty most important writers of the 20th Century by his fellow professional writers in the same year. His 1997 novel, *Tallgrass*, (Bantam) was chosen as a Book-of-the-Month Club selection, and his next, *Medicine Hat*, (Oklahoma Press) as a Doubleday Book Club choice. Current are *The Long Journey Home*, (Forge) and *Raven Mocker* (Oklahoma University Press.)

He is a popular speaker and lecturer on the Great Plains, and the lore and literature of the American West, and is a member of the Speakers' Bureau for the Kansas Humanities Council. He and his wife, Edna, also maintain a small ranching operation, and have raised cattle, Appaloosa horses, and five daughters, not necessarily in that order.